PRELUDE TO SCIENCE

An Exploration of Magic and Divination

ALSO BY RICHARD FURNALD SMITH

Chemistry for the Million

RICHARD FURNALD SMITH

PRELUDE
TO
SCIENCE

An Exploration of Magic and Divination

DRAWINGS BY ANNE CORROUGH

CHARLES SCRIBNER'S SONS / NEW YORK

Library of Congress Cataloging in Publication Data
Smith, Richard Furnald.
    Prelude to science.
    Includes bibliographical references and index.
    1. Occult sciences. I. Title.
    BF1411.S656   133   75-17959
    ISBN 0-684-14370-4

1 3 5 7 9 11 13 15 17 19   v/c   20 18 16 14 12 10 8 6 4 2

PRINTED IN THE UNITED STATES OF AMERICA

CONTENTS

CONTENTS

PREFACE

THE title of this book requires explanation. Magic and divination certainly flourished before science, but they are still with us. They have refused to be swept away by modern science in all its majesty. So if they constitute a prelude, it is a Wagnerian one, introducing themes that recur and evolve throughout the scientific opera that has followed.

The explosion of literature on the occult might be expected to produce a wider range of opinion in this area. But while the levels of scholarship and charm vary, the attitudes expressed tend to remain the same: the reader is still forced to choose between uncritical acceptance and total rejection, even though he feels that both are wrong. His faith in science may be too well grounded to enable him to read a naive occultist without embarrassment, yet he knows that science deals with only a part of his experience and interests.

Perhaps future readers will be able to shop around in occult literature for the exact blend of reason and unreason that suits them. For today's reader, this book provides material he can use in formulating his own blend.

He is urged to take an empirical approach. Ample references are supplied for further study. He is encouraged to investigate and experiment. Magic and divination can be the objects of scientific study. However, they are not in themselves scientific, and therefore some authorities claim that they cannot have any value. To safeguard the reader against this kind of reasoning, I have tried to define the boundaries of science as closely as possible and have acknowledged the presence of values on both sides of those boundaries. I then proceed to an overview of magic, a historical survey of divination, and a more detailed discussion of their most widespread and enduring forms: astrology, the Kabbalah, and Tarot. Thereafter the reader is on his own.

PRELUDE TO SCIENCE

An Exploration of Magic and Divination

ONE

Prelude to What?

Science is so old, it has undergone so many changes in its history, it is so linked at every point with other social activities, that any attempted definition, and there have been many, can only express more or less inadequately one of its aspects, often a minor one, that it has had at some period of its growth.

J. D. Bernal, *Science in History*

For an ancient Roman, the word *scire* meant to know, *sciens* meant having knowledge, and *scientia* meant knowledge itself. The need for a word describing people who produce science was not felt until the nineteenth century, when the remarkable English philosopher and mathematician William Whewell invented "scientist" to be used for "a cultivator of science in general." [1]

Scientist is a hybrid word, half Latin and half Greek: *scientia* plus -ιστης (*-istes*), the agent. Whewell invented other words, however, which are just as indispensable and at the same time blamelessly pure 100-percent Greek: eocene, anode, cathode, physicist, ion.

The Greek word for science was, and is, ἐπιστήμη (*epistēmē*), which lingers in English only in "epistemology," a branch of metaphysics which studies the nature and validity of human knowledge.

(3)

It is the kind of word whose meaning one is apt to forget twenty-fours hours after having looked it up.

Since science and art are traditionally opposed, it is a confusing irony that the Greek word for art is τέχνη (*technē*), as in technology. This is the word that Aristotle uses when discussing the writer's "art," that Plato uses in the *Republic* when warning against the seductions of "art." It is in the motto of the physician Hippocrates, more familiar in its Latin version:

Ὁ βίος βραχυς, ἡ δὲ τέχνη μακρὴ

Vita brevis, ars longa.

Life [is] short, art [is] long.

The key difference between science and art is that science emphasizes theoretical knowledge and understanding, while art is more concerned with practical skills and specific products. Viewed this way, τέχνη certainly applies to art—and also to engineering. Unless something about beauty, utility, and purpose is added to the definition, artists cannot be separated from engineers to the satisfaction of both. (Matters are not helped by the fact that *ingénieur* as first used in eighteenth-century France meant architect.)

Artists seem to be much less interested in defining their activities than scientists are: the Penguin *Dictionary of Art and Artists* defines neither art nor artist. Actually artists and engineers both rely on technique, "the ensemble of practices by which one uses available resources in order to achieve certain valued ends." [2]

The aphorism that science is "thinking about the world in the Greek way" [3] is not merely facetious. An excellent case can be made for saying that science began with the Greeks of the seventh century B.C., specifically with Thales of Miletus. The Greeks were the first to turn from percepts (things perceived) to concepts (ideas), to shift their attention from the properties of variously

shaped pieces of farmland to the properties of those shapes themselves. This ability to generalize is an essential characteristic of
science.

"Modern science" is usually said to have begun in the Renaissance, but the basic experimental-inductive method of Sir Francis
Bacon was not established until the seventeenth century. One must
always remember the historical context in which each phase of science's erratic growth took place. "A great part of the mysticism
and superstition of educated man consists of knowledge which has
broken loose from its historical mooring." [4]

Although no definition of science can be entirely successful,
the attempt is instructive and has attracted many agile minds. In
Shakespeare's day, Montaigne wrote: *"La vraie science est une ignorance qui se sait* [True science is an ignorance which knows it-
self]" (*Essais*, II, 12). Although Montaigne uses *science* in the old
sense of all human knowledge, his aphorism implies both fallibility
and self-correction, which gives it a distinctly modern sound.

In the twentieth century a variety of academicians and profes-
sional scientists have tried to catch the eel of science in a definition.
The Nobel prize-winning English physicist Sir George Thomson
began a book with the statement: "Science is essentially a search
for truth." [5] Everyone agrees, but this shifts the problem from defining science to defining truth, which is no easier for us than it was
for Pontius Pilate.

Albert Einstein's famous definition, "The whole of science is
nothing more than a refinement of everyday thinking," [6] echoes
one made a century earlier by the English biologist Thomas Henry
Huxley: "Science is, I believe, nothing but *trained and organized
common sense.*" [7] A similar pragmatic spirit is shown by the con-
temporary English biologist Sir Peter Medawar: "If politics is the
art of the possible, scientific research is surely the art of the soluble." [8]

PRELUDE TO SCIENCE

The American mathematician and philosopher John G. Kemeny works into his definition the *process* by which scientific knowledge is gained: "I shall use the word 'science' to be all knowledge collected by means of the scientific method." He then defines "scientific method" without using the word "science" (no practiced philosopher is going to be caught in a circular definition): "The scientific method is defined by the cycle of induction, deduction, verification, and by its eternal search for improvement of theories which are only tentatively held." [9]

That definition, however, brings in several more terms which must also be defined. The American physicist R. H. Bube takes a simpler approach: "Science is knowledge of the natural world obtained by sense interaction with that world." [10] This defines science by its method and subject matter; it also acknowledges the subjective element in science, something an older tradition tried hard to ignore.

Laymen have their own definition of science, widely accepted and used but seldom recorded. The American chemist and Harvard president James B. Conant once summed this up as: "Science is the activity of people who work in laboratories and whose discoveries have made possible modern industry and medicine." He also gave a definition of his own, which emphasizes the dynamic aspect: "Science is an interconnected series of concepts and schemes that have developed as a result of experimentation and observation and are fruitful of further experimentation and observations." [11]

In science one is forever "getting there," never arriving. Theories can be disproved but never really proved; a high degree of probability is the best one can hope for. The American chemist Gilbert Lewis wrote: "The theory that there is an ultimate truth, although very generally held by mankind, does not seem useful to science except in the sense of a horizon toward which we may proceed, rather than a point which may be reached." [12]

Probably the most heroic definition of all—overloaded, legalistic, and unlovely—was cobbled together for the *Oxford English Dictionary* and sent tottering down the runway in 1933: "Science is a branch of study which is concerned either with a connected body of demonstrated truths or with observed facts systematically classified and more or less colligated by being brought under general laws, and which includes trustworthy methods for the discovery of new truth within its own domain."

By now it must be clear that science can be defined in countless ways, from the most all-embracing to the most restrictive. How science is defined obviously determines what is left outside—the "nonscience."

T W O

Seven Ways of
Not Being Scientific

The real charm of the intellectual life—the life devoted
to erudition, to scientific research, to philosophy, to aes-
thetics, to criticism—is its easiness. It's the substitution of
simple intellectual schemata for the complexities of reality;
of still and formal death for the bewildering movements of
life.

Aldous Huxley, *Point Counter Point*

I f science is simply "knowledge" and art is simply "technique,"
then nearly every human activity is an art, or a science, or
both. And so we have Domestic Science, Christian Science,
and Schools of Secretarial Science on the one hand, and the Art of
Love, the Art of Beer-making, and the Art of Giving Successful
Parties on the other.

At universities, where science departments command enviable
wealth and prestige, many nonsciences have examined themselves
closely and found themselves to be far more scientific than they
had ever imagined. They suddenly "went in for counting something," as the American historian and critic Jacques Barzun noted.[1]
They learned how to use computers and how to get generous

(8)

grants for doing so. Many scholars and artists now display "a pompous jargon, an affectation of method and rigor, and often the pose of Truth's martyr crucified." [2]

Within science itself, each discipline privately considers itself "more scientific" than the others. An anthropologist whose specialty is "the science of the folk tale" does not hesitate to deny full scientific status to psychology and economics. But publicly a traditional pecking order is usually preserved:

physics
chemistry
biology
psychology
anthropology
sociology.

Physicists have their little jokes about chemists, who have their little jokes about biologists, and all three look on the social sciences as cases of arrested development, like alchemy. Even within disciplines there are polarities: "hard" physical biochemists versus "soft" physiological biochemists, "hard" behaviorists versus "soft" Jungians.

Given such an atmosphere, it is difficult and dangerous to draw a line between science and nonscience. The excluded parties tend to become furious. Engineers do not mind, since they make more money than most scientists. Neither do mathematicians, since as custodians of "the language of science" they command the most prestige of all.

If science must be able to conduct reproducible experiments, much of astronomy is a nonscience. If science must make accurate predictions, the study of evolution is a nonscience. The scientific community will not permit these losses, however, so reproducibility and predictability are admired "characteristics" of science, not prerequisites.

For a century a debate has raged over whether history is a "real science." Historians rather think it is. After all, they have banished the anecdote and borrowed freely from anthropology, sociology, and economics. But their biggest success has been in the role of historians of science. Here they can wield influence, criticize, and ride herd on science generally—at least until the philosophers of science catch up with them.

What about disciplines that borrow and adapt methods from several sciences for a limited practical purpose? Kemeny bans criminology from science on the grounds that it lacks "dignity." [3] Even though dignity has not figured in any definition of science, few scientists would quarrel with this verdict.

Rather than argue with a touchy and tenured faculty, some university administrators simply call the physical, natural, and social sciences "science" and everything else "nonscience." I will do the same. Just remember that for the past two centuries the actual boundaries of science have been no more stable than Poland's.

Since few great minds have focused their awful powers on it, there are no aphoristic definitions of nonscience, no precise blueprints of its parts. Even so, a number of useful distinctions can be made.

Nonscience. This is a neutral, purely descriptive word which includes art, literature, music, theater, movies, football, chess, cookery, politics, the law, and religion. Only someone suffering from scientism (as defined later) could find it a term of reproach.

Unscience. The noun "unscience" is used facetiously, but the adjective "unscientific" is roughly equivalent to a pronouncement of anathema in the Middle Ages. Procedures that fall short of the methods and principles of science and disciplines whose claims have been proved false—or whose claims are so stated that they cannot be proved false—are excommunicated by means of this word. Phrenology, astrology, and the phlogiston theory remain classic examples of unscience, despite some interesting attempts to rehabilitate them.

Pseudoscience. The Greek prefix ψευδ (false, lying) introduces a note of deliberate fraud. The failure to achieve scientific standards is not due to ignorance or inability but to the desire to give a false impression. In the early 1960s, an American pharmaceutical house systematically falsified laboratory data in order to continue marketing a dangerously toxic but profitable drug.[4] There was no shortage of scientific knowledge or equipment in the research laboratories of this firm, just a shortage of honesty.

Quasi-Science. When the props and language of science are used to adorn a basically unscientific activity, the result is something that looks like science (*quasi* = resembling) but is not. Quasi-science may overlap pseudoscience, and in journalistic usage the two terms are sometimes equated, but the distinction between them is real. The more impressive forms of medical quackery are probably the best examples, although one is tempted to include market analysis and weather prediction.

Anti-Science. There have always been people who maintain that science is wicked and false—the enemy. Since science is too huge and protean for anyone to attack in its entirety, some particularly hateful aspect (evolution, the germ theory of disease) is singled out for the main onslaught. Many legislators are more interested in protecting future generations from Darwin than from pollution.

Fundamentalist Christian sects, homeopathy, Culpeper herbalism provide obvious instances, but antagonism to science is more broadly based. Scientific societies recognize and fret over the growing irrationalism: "Many of the intelligentsia seem bent on excluding any understanding of science and technology from their cerebrations. Consequently, basic forces in our world are treated as magical, awesome, or demonic." [5]

When people say they are "against science," they may only be against the exploitation of science by nonscientists. A research scientist working for the government, a corporation, or even a university signs away all rights to any discoveries he makes. His employers determine how the products of his research will be used, what safeguards (if any) will be taken, and just how much damage they will be permitted to cause the people and the environment.

Scientism. The word "scientism" was derived innocently enough from Whewell's "scientist," but over the years it has gained an increasingly derogatory meaning. Now it refers to an uncritical idolization of science—the belief that only science can solve human problems, that only science has value. "Scientism divides all thought into two categories: scientific thought and nonsense." [6] Some people claim that scientism is limited to overenthusiastic laymen. Yet such respected scientists as Jacques Monod, B. F. Skinner, Konrad Lorenz, and Desmond Morris have been described as "scientism's most visible and influential practitioners." [7]

Inability to find value or significance outside one's own work is a common occupational hazard. Small minds display such inability proudly; they claim they have ruthlessly sacrificed all distracting talents to achieve it. Upon closer examination, one usually finds either that they had no distracting talents, or that the results were not worth the sacrifice. Larger minds regard it as an affliction. Charles Darwin wrote in his old age: "If I had to live my life again I would have made a rule to read some poetry and listen to some music at least once every week; for perhaps the parts of my brain now atrophied could thus have been kept active through use. The loss of these tastes is a loss of happiness." [8]

Pre-Science. Before the flowering of modern science, magical strategies were abundant and varied. The Scottish anthropologist Sir James Frazer theorized that human thought progressed "from magic through religion to science" (a sequential relationship he somewhat confused by calling magic "the bastard sister of science"). [9]

The French psychologist Lucien Lévy-Bruhl echoed Frazer when he suggested that primitive man indulged in "pre-logical thought," which he described as mystical, emotional, and not embarrassed by contradictions. [10] The weight of anthropological evidence today, however, favors the view that pre-logical thought develops concurrently with logical thought and is never completely displaced by it. The Belgian anthropologist Claude Lévi-Strauss has suggested that magic and science are "two parallel modes of acquiring knowledge." [11]

The title "Prelude to Science" implies that pre-science will be the main subject of this book. Most histories of science begin with the Paleolithic toolmakers, however. Since a prelude to Paleolithic thought is not intended, "pre-science" must be redefined here as "before modern science"—that is, before about 1650.

The seven types of nonscience described above are by no means mutually exclusive. Each has been applied to astrology at some time. Astrology has also been classified as a science, as an art, and even, by American astrologer Sydney Omarr, as "a scientific art."

A final point: not every published piece of scientific research is a gold mine of scientific thinking. The Polish-born English sociologist Stanislav Andreski writes, "95% of research is indeed re-search for things that have been found long ago and many times since." [12] Much published research in the physical sciences is the work of technicians or automated instruments; while it may be useful or necessary, the type of thought behind it is roughly the same as that required for filing.

Nor is scientific thinking by any means restricted to science. An article on rococo art by a critic like Michael Levey is likely to contain more scientific thinking than the latest chromatographic analysis of pea protein published in a biochemical journal.

THREE

Magic: Premonitions of an Unborn Science?

*Les rites et les croyances magiques apparaitraient alors
comme autant d'expressions d'un acte de foi en une science
encore a naître.*

[Magical rites and beliefs appear as so many expressions
of an act of faith in a science yet to be born.]

Claude Lévi-Strauss, *La Pensée Sauvage*

The thread-waisted wasp (*Sphex*) buries her eggs in the
ground with a freshly stung grasshopper or cricket. Before dragging in the paralyzed insect, she enters the burrow alone to make sure it is safe. If an observer moves the insect
back a few inches from the entrance while she is inspecting the
burrow, she will repeat the entire performance—that is, she will
drag the insect up to the threshold again and make another check
of the burrow. If the insect is moved back forty times, she will repeat the burrow inspection forty times. The wasp is not "thinking"; she is simply following a sequence of inherited behavior patterns.[1]

Born without such "pre-wired" neural patterns, primitive man
had to learn defensive behavior patterns and then transmit them
from generation to generation. The continuity of archaeological

evidence shows how successfully this was done for skills like tool making and fire control. A rudimentary science was created, "a body of public information drawn from the private experiences of individual hominids but somehow imparted to other members of the species."[2]

At the same time, magic and religion were used to account for illnesses, misfortunes, and sudden deaths. Nothing was left unexplained. Rituals were organized around seasonal events and stressful moments in the life cycle. These too were transmitted from generation to generation.

Little distinction was made between science and magic. In the so-called medical papyri of ancient Egypt, magical incantations, rational and irrational prescriptions are all jumbled together. One treatment in the Ebers papyrus (c. 1600 B.C.) has the patient chew caster-oil beans "to clear out all that is in the body"; another advises him to drink the testicles of a black ass crushed and mixed in wine.[3]

Magic and science have at least one goal in common: control of the natural world. Magic makes use of observation, systems of classification, even experimentation. But while magic is just as interested in practical results as science is, it is much less interested in discovering and testing causes. It is far more tolerant of failure, partly because its aims are far more grandiose. An alchemist following a recipe for making gold would not complain of a thousand failures if he had one success. A chemist following a recipe for making aspirin demands success each time.

In the past, science was subservient to priests and magicians on the one hand, craftsmen and artisans on the other. Only in the seventeenth and eighteenth centuries did it win independent status. Slowly and painfully, chemistry detached itself from alchemy, astronomy from astrology, pharmacology from herbalism. Today science tends to be subservient to government and business, though there are some notable exceptions.

Magic: Premonitions of an Unborn Science?

Scientists have varied attitudes toward their magical past. Most chemists are tolerant—even proud—about alchemy, but astronomers take a hard line toward astrology. Possibly chemists would be less broadminded if they were surrounded by rich alchemists and saw columns of alchemical advice in all the daily papers.

While alchemy today does not begin to rival astrology and herbalism in popularity, some writers claim to find all sorts of scientific and spiritual values in its theories. For example, the authors of *The Case for Astrology* declare that "Organic chemistry is principally concerned with the interaction of four chemical elements: Hydrogen, Carbon, Oxygen, Nitrogen. The *functions* of these elements, the parts they play in organic life, can be shown to correspond neatly to the roles played by Fire, Earth, Air and Water." This statement is followed by a piece of verbal sleight-of-hand which might almost be described as alchemical: "Though imprecise from a scientific point of view, the ancient terminology has the advantage of being more fluid and therefore more easily applicable to the manifold contingencies of life than modern terminology." [4]

In *Maps of Consciousness*, the American psychologist Ralph Metzner, a colleague of Timothy Leary and Richard Alpert during the 1960s, repeats the analogy rather more cautiously: ". . . 99 percent of the atoms of protein, the chief ingredient of living matter, are constituted of the elements carbon, oxygen, hydrogen, and nitrogen. Perhaps this is one aspect of what the alchemists meant by the four elements." Metzner views the alchemists as incredibly wise spiritual leaders. Those who tried to enrich themselves were not "genuine alchemical adepts"—and besides, that's just what modern chemists are trying to do, so how dare they criticize? In a rush of non sequiturs, he links the alchemists' conception of sulfur and salt with modern acid-base regulation, with the hydrogen ion concentration of the blood (which has "an important effect on the psyche"), and with the action of positively and negatively ionized air. He predicts the rise of a new alchemy which will "take into account everything the chemists have learned, and will provide more comprehensive and satisfying formulations." For those unable to wait, he supplies exercises: pretending to be one of the four elements, or trying to experience "alchemical androgynous consciousness." "One minute of such experimental self-observation," he insists, "is worth several hours of reading." [5] One can certainly think of cases where this is true.

Nothing that has come down to us concerning the alchemists supports the view that they were extraordinary spiritual guides or that disciples were illumined by their teachings. Yet many people today benefit from irrational techniques which jar them out of conventional thought patterns. And whatever else they may be, alchemical writings are gloriously irrational.

Magic is usually defined as an "art," or a "pretended art," possibly to avoid having to call it a science. Sympathetic (and cautious) writers call it both an art and a science. Strictly speaking, it is neither. When a group of ancient Romans slaughtered a heifer and studied its liver to learn about future events, it was not science, and it certainly wasn't art.

Magic tries to alter the natural course of events (like science) by compelling the aid of supernatural beings or occult powers (unlike science). It has assumed enough forms to intimidate the most hardened taxonomist. However, most varieties can be grouped under four headings:

Imitative Magic. The desired event is mimicked or dramatized.
Sympathetic Magic. The desired action on a person is performed on something associated with that person—hair, nail clippings, clothes, name, footprints, shadow, portrait.

Ritual Magic. The desired event is compelled by using "words of power" in a precisely detailed ritual.

Divination. Hidden information, usually about the future, is obtained by supernatural means.

Obviously there may be considerable overlapping. In Virgil's eighth Eclogue (first century B.C.), a woman of Thessaly brings about her wandering lover's return through a dramatic ritual involving chants, circling an altar, binding and melting images of the lover, and burying his clothes. If she had asked him for information about the future as well as for love, her spell would have included all four types of magic.

The sophisticated "poetic" magic of Virgil's Eclogue (and the sensuous Idyl II of Theocritus on which it is based) is very different from the crude magic of illiterate societies. Both may be performing the same category of magic, but the psychological climate, the style, and no doubt the results will be dissimilar. Both groups have received a bad press.

"The primitive magician," Frazer wrote from high in his ivory tower, "never analyzes the mental assumptions on which his performance is based, never reflects on the abstract principles involved. With him, as with the vast majority of men, logic is implicit, not explicit; he knows magic only as a practical thing, and to him it is always an art, never a science, the very idea of science being foreign to his thinking." [6] And the Polish anthropologist Bronislaw Malinowski stated: "Primitive magic—every field anthropologist knows it to his cost—is extremely monotonous and unexciting, strictly limited in its means of actions, circumscribed in its beliefs, stunted in its fundamental assumptions." [7]

Nevertheless, primitive magic may actually "work." It may have undergone a kind of natural selection and have survival value for its users.

The medicine men (*sikerei*) of the Mentawei Islands west of Sumatra treat patients suffering from diarrhea by having them lie face down on the edge of a cliff and periodically lick the earth. A cure usually follows. The cliff is made out of kaolin, the absorbent clay found in commercial diarrhea remedies such as Kaopectate.[8]

The spring sacrifice to insure crop fertility is an extremely ancient kind of agricultural magic. Primitive societies in Africa, Indo-China, the Philippines, Bengal, and Latin America have slaughtered human victims and buried pieces of their bodies in cultivated fields. The writer and director Pier Pasolini vividly re-created such a rite in his 1969 film *Medea*, to make the heroine's later actions more plausible. As late as the eighteenth century the Pawnee Indians in midwestern North America used to sacrifice a young girl before each spring planting, sprinkling the planted corn kernels with her blood.[9] The Indians that the Pilgrims encountered when they landed at Plymouth in 1620, had scaled this custom down to burying a fish in each hill of corn planted.[10] Organic fertilizers have had a long history.

When game is scarce, the Labrador Indians resort to a form of divination known as scapulimancy—heating animal bones and interpreting the cracks that develop. They heat the shoulderblade of a caribou over coals, then use the resulting cracks to show the route their hunting parties are to follow. This "randomizing" technique gives better results than their usual policy of hunting in areas of past success, where game may now be absent. It is thought to be a significant factor in the tribe's continued survival.[11]

As for the more civilized practitioners of magic, E. M. Butler, professor of German at Cambridge University, dismissed them as "a small group of eccentric or hysterical or neurotic or decadent persons." [12] No doubt some were. A more common complaint has been the pervasive mediocrity. One cannot read very much in the literature of the occult and the supernatural without being struck by how commonplace, how devoid of the least hint of illumination or spiritual insight, are the thoughts and purposes expressed. Members of the Hermetic Order of the Golden Dawn in the 1890s wore gorgeous costumes and brandished magic wands in incense-filled sanctuaries, yet one initiate recalls, "I was oppressed by the drab appearance of my fellow mystics . . . the very essence of the British middle-class." [13]

The same banality extends to conversations with the dead. In 1854, Victor Hugo contacted Shakespeare at a seance. "Are you going on with your work?" Hugo asked, using the familiar *tu* form. Shakespeare claimed to prefer the French language and favored Hugo with some pious verses in which he ordered his characters to genuflect before God (*"Hamlet, Lear, à genoux! À genoux, Romeo!"*).[14]

Thomas Huxley found the triteness of messages from the spirit world a powerful argument against suicide: "Better to live a crossing-sweeper than die and be made to talk twaddle by a 'medium' hired at a guinea a *séance*." [15]

How the message arrives is everything; the message itself, nothing.

P. E. I. Bonewits, who received a B.A. in magic from the University of California in 1970, has called magic the active aspect of occultism, mysticism its passive aspect.[16] But religious contemplation is by no means a passive condition, and its literature is filled with warnings against "quietism." The difference is more fundamental. The mystical traditions of the major religions condemn magic as a distraction, a trap, something to be bypassed as quickly as possible. Qualities that are considered major obstacles by mystics, such as egomania and will power, seem always to have been the prime requisites for practicing magicians.

Apparently some people have been able to shift back and forth between miracle working and contemplation. Perhaps it is enough not to attempt both at the same time.

Writing just after this century's major magician, Aleister

Crowley (1875–1947), died in England, E. M. Butler stated: "The times were against him. There were much more potent, dangerous, destructive and evil personalities about, who have produced disasters on a scale of such magnitude as to make *The Book of the Law* seem vapid and the writer's influence on the life of his age utterly negligible." [17]

Thirty years later Crowley's influence is far from negligible. Many of his experiments in magic were unbelievably silly and nonproductive, but he recorded them and has kept many from making the same mistakes. The defects of his mind and character are no secret—they are broadcast throughout his works. Yet he remains a useful case history, a time-saving teacher, and a cautionary example to today's serious occultists. Empirical magicians such as Bonewits are quick to acknowledge their debt to him.

Anthropologists have long studied primitive magic and participated in tribal rituals—rather in the spirit of Anna Russell's clubwoman, "not expecting either reward or enjoyment." Weston La Barre ate peyote with the Indians in the 1930s for his Ph. D. thesis. But he denounced Havelock Ellis, Aldous Huxley, and other "British eaters" as "ethnologically spurious, meretricious and foolish poseurs" [18]—apparently for eating peyote without the proper clinical attitude; that is, for behaving like natives, rather than like students of natives.

Anything can be the object of scientific study, however. No matter how "spurious," "decadent," or "negligible" its practitioners, civilized magic is a reality and deserves to be studied along with the primitive.

In all cultures, from the most primitive to the most sophisticated, the most viable type of magic is divination.

FOUR

Divination: Who Knows What the Future Will Bring?

καὶ τὰ δοκηθέντ' οὐκ ἐτελέζθη,
τῶν δ'ἀδοκήτων πόρον ηὖρε θεός
[The things we expected—don't happen;
The unexpected—God brings about].

Euripides, *Medea* (author's translation)

Lord, we know what we are, but know not what we may be.

Shakespeare, *Hamlet*

The novelist E. M. Forster imagined early storytelling as a group of cave men sitting around a fire and listening open-mouthed to the tribal narrator. Crude suspense mesmerized them, making them ask over and over again: "And what happened next? . . . And then? . . . And then? . . ." [1]

In most fiction the answers to such questions come thick and fast and bring a special pleasure to the reader, perhaps because in real life he is continually making decisions based on inadequate information and never really knows what will happen next. People are always looking for more data—anything that will help them see the future more clearly. Whatever promises to do this—astrology, market analysis, coin tossing—will be welcomed somewhere by someone. It does not always have to be right. Even 50 percent accuracy is better than total ignorance.

Given this need and given the extraordinary ability of the human mind to make sense out of things, it is natural occasionally to make sense out of things that have no sense at all—random events, coincidences, far-fetched analogies—and to overinterpret them and force them into a statement about the future, even an incorrect one.

Divination refers to obtaining "hidden knowledge" about anything—not just about the future. Thus it includes water witching (the technique of locating underground water by supernatural means) and obtaining hidden treasure by means of spirits, a popular hobby in the Middle Ages. Compared with the difficulties of turning lead into gold and finding the secret of eternal youth, locating a treasure already in existence must have seemed more modest and feasible. Medieval magical books give detailed instructions and the names of helpful spirits to be invoked. The *Lemegeton* ("Lesser Key") of Solomon lists nine such spirits. One of them, Amy, also gives astrology lessons.[2]

Omens have always been searched for and found in the flights of birds, the rustling of trees, crystal balls, tea-leaves, palms, cards, dreams, casting lots, opening a book at random, listening to seashells. In the fourth century B.C., according to the Greek scholar Polyaenus, the entire Athenian army refused to embark for a crucial battle because someone sneezed.

Natural pedantry and a desire to dignify the subject matter has produced a polysyllabic term for each kind of divination: rhabdomancy (water witching), oneiromancy (dream interpretation), chiromancy (palmistry), metoposcopy (mole interpretation). Pedantic classification schemes also abound. The *Encyclopaedia Britannica* in its fourteenth edition (1972) divides the subject into Internal Methods and External Methods, according to whether the message comes from within the seeker (dreams) or from some specific outer event (astrology).

This seems to be a clumsy and uncredited borrowing from Cicero (106–43 B.C.), who divided the subject into Natural Divination (the dreams and prophecies of persons divinely inspired) and Artificial Divination (the study of omens, stars, bird flights, and so forth by experienced observers).[3] Cicero must have noticed the gulf between the divine frenzies of a priestess of Apollo and his own cold and bureaucratic activities as state augur. So he separated the inspired seers from politicians like himself. His distinction was based on talent, for some individuals do have a genuine, measurable talent for divination. The methods are of secondary importance; they are merely props, or ways of focusing attention.

In its fifteenth edition (1974), the *Britannica* gives Cicero his due and adds a third type to the scheme—"interpretive divination," where both formal procedure and special insight are involved.

ORACLES IN THE ANCIENT WORLD

Craving for foreknowledge is found in our earliest literature. The Bible mentions at least twenty ways of getting information about the future. Probably the most spectacular is the raising of Samuel by the Witch of Endor, to answer questions about the next day's battle with the Philistines (I Samuel, 28). At King Saul's command, the nervous witch conjures up the aged prophet, who angrily predicts Saul's ruin. This chronicle was written about 1000 B.C. and is paralleled by an episode in the *Odyssey* (c. 750

B.C.) in which Odysseus coaxes the prophet Tiresias up from the underworld with a trough of sheeps' blood (Book 11). Once again the purpose is information about the future.

Necromancy (νεκρός, corpse + μαντεία, divination) is a rather drastic way of getting information, and the raised dead always complain. So simpler methods were developed for daily use. Oracles kept the ancient world supplied with answers for century after century. With no sacred text to rely on, the Greeks and Romans could still feel they were receiving divine guidance. The oracles at Delphi, Dodona, and Ammon were the most influential, but scores of lesser oracles operated successfully.

The most ancient of the three was the oracle at Dodona, in a wild and mountainous part of northwestern Greece. Here Zeus transmitted messages through the rustlings of a sacred oak, which were interpreted by the Selli, "whose feet are unwashed and who sleep on the ground" (*Iliad*, Book 16). Pottery remains suggest that Dodona was the site of a Neolithic sky-god cult. Like the sacred oak itself, the priests maintained contact with the earth and obtained special powers thereby.

The method at Dodona shifted (perhaps with the death of the sacred oak) to simple yes-or-no answers obtained by lot. When the Spartans visited the oracle in 371 B.C. to learn if they would win their war with Thebes, the pet ape of the king of Molossi ran amuck in the sanctuary, overturning all the sacred paraphernalia. The angry priestess told them to forget about victory and think about saving their skins.[4]

The oracle of Delphi, probably the most famous, was apparently influenced by Mycenaean civilization and formed part of an earth-goddess cult. The legend of Apollo's taking charge of the oracle after killing a serpent sacred to the goddess may refer to the change of religions that occurred when the northern Greek invaders defeated the original inhabitants. Even so, Apollo's official mouthpiece at Delphi, the Pythia, remained female.

Divination: Who Knows What the Future Will Bring?

Although it was a strong unifying force in the early days of Greece, the Delphic oracle was politically reactionary and not always above bribery. It preached appeasement during the Persian War, switching sides in the nick of time, and it was anti-Athenian for most of the Peloponnesian War.

The oracle of Ammon, located at an oasis 200 miles in the Libyan desert, was another yes-or-no-style oracle. But it declared Alexander the Great a god when he visited it in 331 B.C. Because of its remoteness, it was probably the last oracle to cease operations as Christianity spread through the Mediterranean. By the fourth century A.D. all of the oracles had fallen silent, and not even the Emperor Julian could revive them. Christians carried out the destruction of oracle sites with particular thoroughness.

"Divination" is a far more grand and serious term than "fortune-telling." It echoes back to ancient Rome where an extraordinary amount of time was spent, publicly and privately, searching omens and portents for clues to the future. "*Si dii sint,*" wrote Cicero, "*sit divinatio*" [If the gods exist, divination exists].[5]

As a state augur (*aves gero*, bird carrier), Cicero himself studied the flight of birds and then reported whether the auspices (*aves spicio*, bird inspection) were favorable or unfavorable. From the Etruscans, the Romans learned haruspication, the art of reading the future in the livers of sacrificed animals. An active belief in witchcraft, talismans, miracles, and of course astrology flourished in all social classes. Juvenal, at about 100 A.D., showed how much divination was part of the domestic scene in his Sixth Satire (marvelously translated by John Dryden in 1693). He pictures a wife consulting Armenian fortune-tellers, dove lungs, and puppy entrails to learn of new love affairs or bequests, then visiting a jail-bird astrologer:

> From him your Wife enquires the Planets' Will,
> When the black Jaundice shall her Mother kill:

PRELUDE TO SCIENCE

Her Sister's and her Uncle's end would know;
But first, consults his Art, when *you* shall go.

Some towns in the Roman Empire harbored so many different religions and cults (according to Petronius) that they actually must have contained more gods than men. All these beliefs and superstitions "were considered by the people as equally true, by the philosopher as equally false, and by the magistrate as equally useful." [6]

Not that Rome was uniquely irrational by any means; it had simply become a clearing house for most of the world's superstitions. But not all of them.

THE *I CHING*

In China, scapulimancy (mentioned earlier as being used by Labrador Indians) evolved into the *I Ching* (Book of Changes), a divinatory system so complete and satisfying in itself that science was allegedly neglected because of it.

Many of the ideas and attitudes of ancient China are embodied in the *I Ching*, and one tends to absorb them while using it as an oracle. This, along with the *I Ching*'s great age and extraordinary viability, makes it a rewarding object of study. C. F. Baynes's English translation of Richard Wilhelm's German translation is still the most popular and complete, although the version by English occultist Alfred Douglas (*The Oracle of Change*) is a useful low-priced alternative.[7]

The interplay of the two forces, yin (female, negative, receptive, dark) and yang (male, positive, active, bright) is the basis of the *I Ching*. In nature, the yin force is maximum at the winter solstice, while the yang force is maximum at the summer solstice.

The two forces are equal at the spring and fall equinoxes. Yin also represents earth, while yang is the sky or heaven. In the *I Ching*, yin is shown by a broken line (— —) and yang is shown by an unbroken line (———).

Yin and yang lines can be combined in sets of three, called trigrams. The eight (2^3) possible combinations have traditional names and attributes:

Earth (receptive)	Mountain (immovable)	Water (dangerous)	Wind (gentle)
Thunder (arousing)	Fire (clinging)	Lake (joyful)	Heaven (active)

When yin and yang lines are combined in sets of six, the figures are called hexagrams. There are sixty-four (2^6) possible combinations. The name and meaning of each hexagram is more or less derived from the two trigrams of which it is made. Hexagram 20, Contemplation, consists of Wind (gentle) over Earth (receptive):

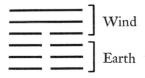 Wind

Earth

The hexagrams that are obtained when the trigram Earth is combined with itself and with each of the seven other trigrams in turn follow.

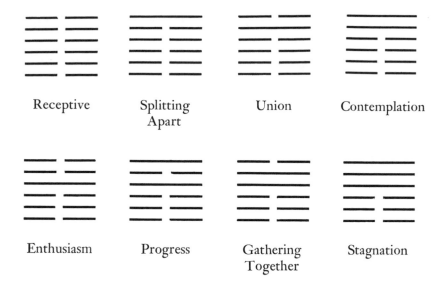

| Receptive | Splitting Apart | Union | Contemplation |

| Enthusiasm | Progress | Gathering Together | Stagnation |

The *I Ching* consists of detailed descriptions of each of the sixty-four hexagrams. To consult the oracle, one formulates the question and casts yarrow stalks or coins six times to obtain a hexagram. One then studies the meaning of the hexagram in the *I Ching*.

The yarrow stalk method is slow and complicated and requires fifty stalks of yarrow (*Achillea millefolium*), one to two feet long. Serious students prefer it, because it favors concentration and discourages trivial questions. The more commonly used method requires three Chinese coins, inscribed on one side, plain on the other. The inscribed side is yin and has a value of two; the plain side is yang and has a value of three. Each time the coins are thrown, one of the following will result:

2 + 2 + 2 = 6 (an Old Yin line)   —— —— *
2 + 2 + 3 = 7 (a Young Yang line)   ————
2 + 3 + 3 = 8 (a Young Yin line)   —— ——
3 + 3 + 3 = 9 (an Old Yang line)   ———— *

By throwing the coins six times one builds a hexagram from the bottom (line 1) to the top (line 6). The Old Yin and Old Yang lines (indicated by asterisks) are sometimes called "active" or "moving" lines and have special significance. The *I Ching* gives additional meanings for such lines. They are also considered to be unstable, so a second hexagram must be drawn with the "moving" lines reversed (Old Yin lines changed into Young Yang lines, Old Yang lines turned into Young Yin lines). For example, if one obtained 8, 8, 8, 7, 7, 9, one would have hexagram 12, Stagnation. The "moving" sixth line carries the message that stagnation is about to end. Reversed, the sixth line gives hexagram 45, Gathering Together:

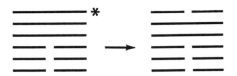

This suggests a state of inertia on the point of being favorably resolved. On the other hand, if one had obtained 8, 6, 8, 7, 7, 7, one would again draw hexagram 12, Stagnation, but with a "moving" second line which reverses to give hexagram 6, Conflict:

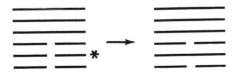

This suggests inertia leading to a fight.

The *I Ching* usually depicts an ever-shifting situation where nothing, good or bad, lasts forever. The language used is rich, varied, and sufficiently vague to encourage the questioner to "make sense of it" in terms of his current preoccupations. Anyone who enjoys the works of Lao-tse, Chuang-tse, and Confucius will find his opinions subtly reinforced by the *I Ching;* others may find that these writers become accessible to them for the first time. Intuitive religious teachers like Stephen Gaskin, founder of "The Farm" commune in Tennessee, find an entire course of spiritual enlightenment built into it.[8]

Disarming truthfulness is the impression its answers most often convey. "The *I Ching* doesn't send you valentines," as author Ken Kesey once remarked.[9] Some occultists find this offensive. Even Confucius is reported to have been miffed by one of its answers. Literal-minded persons tend to have trouble with the *I Ching;* in one case a questioner took the recurrent phrase "great good fortune" to mean a large cash inheritance and became furious when one did not instantly materialize.

On occasion the *I Ching* can be flattering, which may be a factor in its survival. Carl Jung wrote a warmly sympathetic foreword to the Wilhelm translation; his first response was "The Cauldron," suggesting that he was a dispenser of wisdom and civilized refinements to a grateful society. One wonders what kind of foreword he would have written if his response had been "Work on What Has Been Spoiled." My first response from the *I Ching* was "The Creative," which I did not find hard to take.

The sixty-four hexagrams are remarkably generalized, so that they cover most basic human situations. Answers usually contain something the questioner finds meaningful. The *I Ching* is totally without malice. Questions asked with hostile intent tend to receive nonsensical answers. Aleister Crowley reported that he found the *I Ching* always reliable, whereas Tarot cards might give spiteful and deceptive answers or play practical jokes.[10]

Unlike Tarot cards (which are discussed in chapter 10), *I Ching* hexagrams do not lend themselves to use in curses or spells for personal gain. They function like a kindly but shrewd uncle with a rich store of sensible and morally safe advice. How many psychotherapists do as well?

If the *I Ching* becomes so fascinating in itself that people neglect to study the real world or correct social abuses, then it is indeed "a mischievous handicap," which is what the English biochemist and orientalist Joseph Needham called it after tracing its influence on the development of science in China.[11] Certainly monomania of any kind is a very real danger. Today the *I Ching* hardly seems likely to stunt anyone's intellectual development, however, if only because far more efficient distractions and *voleurs des énergies* are freely available.

THE FUTURE OF DIVINATION

Is reliance on divination merely a primitive phase in human development, to be replaced by science and logic? Most of us were taught so. We were also taught that the economy would expand forever and that medical science would eventually wipe out disease.

The economic myth needs no comment here. The French-American microbiologist René Dubos has argued that human disease can never be eliminated, since the genetic variability which insures our survival is shared by the pathogenic organisms which attack us.[12] The psychologist Gustav Jahoda now suggests that people can never be completely educated out of superstition, because "superstition is an integral part of the adaptive mechanisms without which humanity would be unable to survive."[13]

Divination and the "occult arts" thrive under conditions of insecurity: wars, plagues, natural disasters, and political upheavals. The riskiest professions—acting, gambling, the military—are also the most universally superstitious. Malinowski observed that, in the Trobriand Islands, natives who lived in villages on sheltered lagoons had no magic connected with fishing, while natives who lived in villages on the open sea where fishing was dangerous and yields unpredictable had elaborate rituals associated with it. These and other studies led him to theorize that man uses magic only in those areas "where chance and circumstances are not fully controlled by knowledge" and that man could not have advanced to higher levels of culture without it. "Magic . . . enables man to carry out with confidence his important tasks, to maintain his poise and his mental integrity in fits of anger, in the throes of hate, of unrequited love, of despair and anxiety." [14] The theory can even be treated quantitatively in some cases. A study of water witching in the United States shows that the difficulty of locating ground water in a given area is directly proportional to the number of water witchers in that area. The authors conclude that water witching is a ritual which "reduces anxiety" in these rural communities just as magic does in pre-literate societies.[15]

If a magical procedure can reduce anxiety enough to permit effective action, it certainly has positive survival value. Perhaps a kind of natural selection operates, preserving the more successful anxiety-reducers.

A person who receives the Darkening of the Light hexagram from the *I Ching*, or the Death card in a Tarot spread will presumably feel a stab of anxiety at the time but will no doubt be more circumspect that day. The anxiety provoked by a painted playing card is less than that provoked by a real mugger.

More people have devoted more time to astrology than to any other form of divination. Tarot cards are a thousand years more recent, yet they seem to embody enough of man's "collective unconscious" to guarantee their survival. They have blended with the Jewish mystical tradition known as the Kabbalah to form one of the cultural curiosities of this age.

All three have magical as well as divinatory aspects. European witchcraft is unthinkable without astrology (curses are delivered when the moon is waning on a Tuesday, the day of Mars, or a Saturday, the day of Saturn). The legendary Rabbi Loew of Prague brought the Golem to life with a kabbalistic formula. And the working of magical spells with Tarot cards is not limited to certified Gypsies.

Astrology, the Kabbalah, and Tarot will therefore be examined in detail in the remaining chapters.

FIVE

Astrology: Are We Fools by Heavenly Compulsion?

> Fut! I should have been that I am,
> had the maidenliest star in the firmament
> twinkled on my bastardizing.
>
> Shakespeare, *King Lear*

ORIGINS

Thousands of stars are visible in the night sky, forming a complex pattern that shifts silently from east to west and gives hints of underlying order—a cosmic mystery waiting to be solved. Skywatching is surely one of the oldest of human activities. Mesolithic nomads must have used the moon and the stars to find their way across unmarked terrain.

In predynastic Egypt (5000–3200 B.C.) the rising of the brightest star, Sirius, forecast the annual flooding of the Nile and the start of the agricultural cycle. Bronze-age sailors navigated by the stars, and great Neolithic structures like Stonehenge were carefully aligned with astronomical events.

Astronomers accept the idea that astronomy "grew out" of astrology. ("Since astrologers kept a very careful record of the motions of the sky for superstitious predictions," states the *Dictionary of Astronomical Terms*, "a technique of observation was developed which was later applied to astronomy." [1]) Yet from the surviving evidence it would be easier to prove the reverse position.

"Star catalogues" dating back to 1800 B.C. have been found in Mesopotamia. From 1000 B.C. on, the Babylonians kept such complete and accurate astronomical records that they were able to predict conjunctions, the rising and setting of constellations, retrograde motions of planets, lunar eclipses, and at least the possibility of solar eclipses. The primary goal was the devising of a reliable official calendar. From the government's point of view, it was important to fix the dates of religious festivals and tax collections. From the farmer's point of view, it was important to know when to sow crops.

Boundary stones (*kuddurus*) in the shape of Scorpio, Capricorn, and other signs of the zodiac have been found dating from

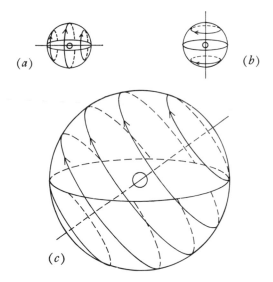

Star movements: (*a*) at the equator; (*b*) at the North Pole; (*c*) in northern latitudes

Sirius, in Canis Major, rising in the east

1000 B.C., but one must remember that while "zodiac" means astrology to us, to the ancients it was merely a circle of familiar constellations marking the agricultural year. Like most ancient peoples, the Babylonians searched for—and found—omens wherever they looked, including the sky. They kept records of plagues, earthquakes, wars and crop failures, and tried to correlate them with eclipses and other celestial events. But nothing more. There are no claims that the stars control individual destiny. There are no individual horoscopes.

Hundreds of reports made to the kings of Babylon and Assyria by priestly astrologers have survived and been widely translated. They state, for example, that a coming lunar eclipse is bad for the Hittites, or that the appearance of a certain planet in a certain constellation will cause "great wrath." The role of these priests and omen readers is clear in the fulminations of the prophet Isaiah:

> Come down and sit in the dust, oh virgin daughter of Babylon. . . . Let now the astrologers and the stargazers, the monthly prognosticators, stand up and save thee. . . . Behold, they shall be as stubble, the fire shall burn them.
>
> Isaiah 47: 1, 13, 14

By the time the Book of Daniel was written (c. 165 B.C.), the royal stargazers had come to seem much less formidable. King Nebuchadnezzar found Daniel "ten times better than all the magicians and astrologers that were in all his realm" (Daniel 1:20).

The use of stars to forecast events affecting nations or large groups of people is called "mundane astrology," which is not what most of us mean by astrology. The average person thinks of astrology as the study of individual birth charts or horoscopes: "natal astrology." Yet out of the vast storehouse of Mesopotamian records less than twenty horoscopes have been found.[2] The earliest of these is dated 409 B.C., a fairly advanced point in ancient history. By then, Babylonia and Assyria were mere provinces of the Persian Empire, the Golden Age of Greece was coming to a tragic end, and the expanding Roman Republic was already a century old.

Stargazing methods from Babylon were exported in the sixth century B.C. to a declining Egypt and to Greece, where astronomy was more scientific but technically less skilled. Nearly 200 Greek horoscopes survive; the earliest is dated 61 B.C.[3] Most of them were made in the first two centuries A.D. Astrology "as we know it" was largely the creation of Macedonian Greeks living in Alexandria. The entire system was codified in the second century A.D. by Claudius Ptolemy, a Greek astronomer born in Upper Egypt.

This means that two recurrent images in popular history are false. In the first, wise Babylonian priests are pictured, not just as stargazing in their ziggurats from 3000 B.C. on, but as practicing advanced astronomy and plotting intricate horoscopes for "untold ages." In the second, the rational Greeks are seen as protecting the West from the superstitious East. The Irish Professor of Classics Benjamin Farrington summed it up in a memorable sentence: "We had a picture of this age-old Chaldean superstition being held in check by Greek rationalism and the sturdy commonsense of Rome until, with the flooding in of eastern peoples, the Orontes emptied into the Tiber and the clear perspectives of the classical landscape were submerged by oriental slime." [4]

CELESTIAL CALENDAR-MAKING

Before plunging into astrological detail, we must examine the more basic subject of how the sun, moon, and stars have always been studied and used by man to orient himself in time.

The sun creates the seasons—in most parts of the world that is obvious enough. After midwinter in the northern hemisphere the days grow longer, and the sun follows a higher path across the sky, so that the radiant energy reaching the earth increases each day both in duration and intensity. Then after the summer solstice the process is reversed.

The solar year, this cyclic waxing and waning of solar energy, determines the course of life on earth. It is marked by four natural

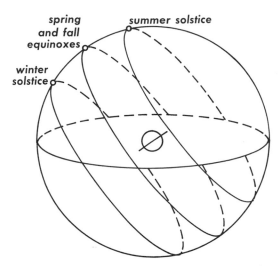

spring
and fall
equinoxes

summer solstice

winter
solstice

The sun's movements in northern latitudes

turning points (τροπαί, *tropai*), which divide the year into four seasons:

winter solstice   (shortest day)
spring equinox   (day and night equal)
summer solstice   (longest day)
fall equinox   (day and night equal)

When a way of marking the passage of time within the four seasons was needed, the moon's cycle offered a convenient time unit. Starting with the first visible crescent, the moon "waxes" for 14 days until full, then "wanes" for 14 days until it disappears from the sky: a recurring cycle of twenty-nine to thirty days. The ancient Greeks, Hebrews, Babylonians, Celts, and Germans based their calendar on the lunar month. The Jews, Mohammedans, and Chinese still do. In nearly all languages (including English) the word for month and the word for moon are related or the same: for example, Hebrew, *yerah*; Greek μήν (*men*); Latin, *mensis*.

The first day of the lunar month may vary from place to place, according to the visibility of the first crescent, but in general the system is simple and uniform. Anyone can tell the date in any given month simply by noting the phase of the moon. There is

(41)

one maddening defect, however. The lunar months and the solar year do not come out even. Twelve lunar months are 11 days too short, while thirteen lunar months are 18 days too long.

Some primitive peoples ignored the problem. Others added extra ("intercalary") days or months when they noticed the lunar months were slipping backward with respect to the solar year. In this way the Sumerians (c. 2500 B.C.) made sure that their traditional month of the barley harvest actually occurred when the barley was being harvested.

The Egyptians had three calendars. They began with a lunar religious calendar, which they synchronized in the dynastic age with a civil calendar of twelve 30-day months, plus 5 feast days. Agricultural seasons, however, were tied to the rising of Sirius (Sothis in the Egyptian language) each summer, as this coincided with the annual flooding of the Nile. The Sothic year almost coincided with the solar year, being only 12 minutes longer.

Since the solar year is actually 365¼ days long, the Egyptian civil calendar of 365 days was off by one day every four years, or less than a month a century. But after a few centuries it was noticed that the flooding of the Nile was occurring in later and later months of the civil calendar, and eventually summer religious festivals were being held in the winter. After passing through each of the twelve months, the Nile flooding returned to where it had started 1,460 years ago. Eventually the discrepancy of 12 minutes between the Sothic year and the solar year also began to show up. In 3000 B.C. the rising of Sirius generally preceded the flooding of the Nile, but the rising slipped back more than a week every 1,000 years, so that it finally lost its value as a harbinger.

Further complications were introduced after the conquest of Egypt by Alexander the Great: the Ptolemys insisted on using the Macedonian calendar.

Throughout ancient Greece, the variations in the calendars of individual cities were notorious and the object of much sarcastic comment. Rome, too, had serious problems until Julius Caesar introduced his reformed calendar. At that time (45 B.C.) he had to add 90 days to the year so as to get the months back where they belonged. Like the Egyptians, he used a year of 365 days, but added an extra day every four years, so that the calendar corresponded more closely to the actual solar year of 365¼ days. In 22 B.C. Augustus tried to "fix" the wandering Egyptian calendar witih Julian-style reforms, which were widely resisted.

The Julian calendar was stable, but at the cost of being out of step with the moon. The only lunar calendar that worked successfully was developed in Mesopotamia. Here the months were always 29 or 30 days long and began with the appearance of the crescent moon. With Sumerian and Babylonian refinements, adjustment to the solar year became less haphazard. After the sixth century B.C. it was achieved by inserting seven extra months each nineteen years. The Assyrians (1100 B.C.) and the Persians (539 B.C.) adopted the Babylonian calendar. So did the Jews, when they were exiled to Babylon after the destruction of Jerusalem by Nebuchadnezzar in 586 B.C., and they still retain a modification of it devised by the patriarch Hillel the Second in A.D. 360.[5]

The only nonastronomical element in the calendar is the seven-day week. It came into general use by a coincidence. Mosaic law required the abstinence from work every seventh day, while in the Roman empire astrologers had decided that each day in succession was ruled by one of the seven "planets," which included the sun and moon and the five planets then known. A series of days named for them gradually became established, beginning with the Christian sabbath and ending with the Jewish sabbath, "without official recognition, either civil or ecclesiastical."[6] When the Latin names were translated into Germanic languages, equivalent northern deities were substituted for four of the Roman gods.

dies Solis	Sun	Sunday
dies Lunae	Moon	Monday
dies Martis	Mars (Tiu)	Tuesday
dies Mercurii	Mercury (Woden)	Wednesday
dies Jovis	Jupiter (Thor)	Thursday
dies Veneris	Venus (Freya)	Friday
dies Saturni	Saturn	Saturday

Thus, to the difficulties of coordinating the solar and lunar cycles was added a nonstop series of weekly cycles that has nothing to do with the other elements of the calendar.

CONSTELLATIONS AND CROPS

Since plant growth is tied directly to the solar year, successful farming has always depended on performing such critical tasks as plowing, sowing, pruning, and harvesting at the right time. Farmers have always had to be in step with the solstices and equinoxes of the solar year, whatever the vagaries of the "official" calendar.

One of the most ancient ways of doing this is to link farming operations with the rising and setting of stars and constellations. This tradition, which must have begun in prehistoric times, was fully developed and flourishing in the eighth century B.C. when the Greek poet Hesiod wrote *Works and Days:*

> Begin your harvest when the Pleiades are rising
>   and your plowing when they are setting. . . .
> Winnow grain when powerful Orion first appears. . . .
> Then the star Arcturus rises brilliant at dusk;
>   after him, the swallow appears to men. . . . Before she
>   comes, prune the vines.[7]

Hesiod gives advice on household management, choosing a wife, and scores of other subjects, but along with cautioning the reader not to urinate facing the sun, not to seduce his brother's wife, not to have sex immediately after a funeral, he connects all the activities of the year with astronomical events and with the coming and going of birds and animals.

The basic pattern was the same centuries later in Imperial Rome. Pliny the Elder (23–79 A.D.) devoted most of Book XVIII of his *Natural History* to elaborations on the agricultural year as marked out by the heavens:

> The summer solstice arrives on June 24th on the 8th degree of Cancer (*in octavo parte cancri*). Now begins the time for picking and harvesting the various crops and preparing for the cruel and savage winter. . . .
>
> The right time for wine-making is during the 44 days between the fall equinox and the setting of the Pleiades. After that, it is useless to tar the cold wine-casks.[8]

Although Pliny complained about how hard it was to teach astronomy to *rusticae*, farmers and also navigators were assumed to be especially knowledgeable about the stars. Even ordinary citizens must have recognized the stars as seasonal guideposts. Virgil, Ovid, Caesar, and other Roman writers routinely indicate the time of year by mentioning the Pleiades (in Taurus), Arcturus (in Boötes), Betelgeuse (in Orion), Sirius (in Canis Major), and Vega (in Lyra).

THE ZODIAC

The Greek astronomer Hipparchus (c. 190–120 B.C.) catalogued some 1,000 stars and described 48 constellations, using his

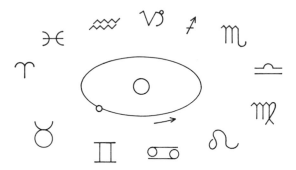

Earth, sun, and zodiac: the sun is shown "in" Scorpio

naked eye and the simplest measuring instruments. Twelve of the constellations received particular attention, because the sun appears to pass through them each year, spending roughly a month in each. These constellations are Aries (the Ram), Taurus (the Bull), Gemini (the Twins), Cancer (the Crab), Leo (the Lion), Virgo (the Virgin), Libra (the Balance), Scorpio (the Scorpion), Sagittarius (the Archer), Capricorn (the Goat), Aquarius (the Water Bearer), and Pisces (the Fishes).

The sun's apparent path as seen from earth is called the ecliptic, since when the moon is on it, eclipses can occur. Each day, the sun appears to move 1 degree east through the fixed stars on the ecliptic. This means that the stars seem to move 1 degree west each day with respect to the sun; if the sun and a given star both "rise" at the same time today on the eastern horizon, the star will rise four minutes ahead of the sun tomorrow, two hours ahead of the sun one month from now.

Since all but one of the constellations on the ecliptic were named after living creatures, taken as a group they were called ζωδιακός κύκλος (*zodiakos kyklos*), circle of little animals. Our names for them are the Latin equivalents of the original Greek: for example, Virgo (virgin) in Greek is παρθένος (*parthenos*), as in parthenogenesis, or virgin birth, and the Parthenon, a temple to the virgin goddess Athena. The Greek names were attributed to Oenopides of Chios (fl. 430 B.C.); he was presumed to have borrowed them from the Babylonians, but this may not be true.

The extent of Babylonian influence on Greek astronomy is uncertain. The Greeks themselves credited the "Chaldeans" with vast astronomical knowledge, a tradition that persisted in Rome, where *chaldeus* was one of the words for "astrologer." But the evidence is extremely sketchy and has been sharply questioned by the English historian D. R. Dicks: "There is, in fact, no real justification for supposing that the similarities are anything other than coincidences between two separately developed constellation systems; until further evidence comes to hand, the Babylonian seems undoubtedly to have been the older, but that is as much as can safely be said." [9]

The zodiac gave the ancient farmer-observer a way of determining exactly where the sun was in its yearly cycle. The lunar months might slip wildly out of place, but a farmer who knew that a certain crop gave the best yield when planted in the fifth degree

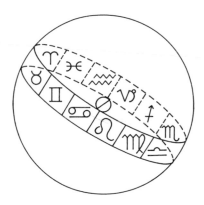

The twelve signs of the zodiac on the ecliptic: ♈ Aries; ♉ Taurus; ♊ Gemini; ♋ Cancer; ♌ Leo; ♍ Virgo; ♎ Libra; ♏ Scorpio; ♐ Sagittarius; ♑ Capricorn; ♒ Aquarius; ♓ Pisces

of Taurus could find that same point year after year, no matter how remote he was from the centers of civilization.

THE STARS AS CAUSES

According to the Greek writer Plutarch (A.D. c.46–c.120), Sirius was called "The Bringer of the Nile" by the Egyptians; they believed that the star not only announced the Nile floods but caused them. Hesiod blamed Sirius for weakening men during the long hot summer:

> In the season of exhausting heat, goats are plumpest, wine is sweetest, and women are most wanton—but men are weakest, because Sirius shrivels them up.[10]

One might have thought that the wine and the women played a part in the shriveling process, but that is not suggested. From the fifth century B.C. on, weather almanacs were compiled in Greece in which certain constellations were associated with certain kinds of weather.

Pliny the Elder was not one of the ancient world's most critical thinkers—he believed that mares were impregnated by the west wind—so he repeats all this weather lore. Sirius causes hot weather; the Hyades (in Taurus) bring "four successive days of bad weather" when they set; Saturn brings rain, and "awful stars" (*horridus sideribus*) such as Arcturus produce hailstones and hurricanes. Crop damage results from blight-producing combinations of moon and stars. While disparaging conventional astrology, Pliny reasoned that, just as the sun affects the earth's seasons, "so each of the stars has its own force and produces effects according to its own nature." [11]

This possibility having been accepted, the way was open to embracing some rather whimsical conclusions. Writing a century after Pliny, Claudius Ptolemy declared that, when "badly placed," Mars and Mercury cause people to be "extravagant, avaricious, savage, venturesome, daring, prone to change their minds, excitable, easily aroused, liars, thieves, blasphemers, perjurers, ready to take the offensive, seditious, lighters of fires, creators of disturbances in theatres, insolent, piratical, burglars, murderers, forgers, villains, wizards, magicans, sorcerers, homicides." [12]

It is a small step from saying a certain event follows the appearance of a star to saying that the star actually causes the event. Though logicians have deplored it for centuries, going from *post hoc* (after this) to *propter hoc* (because of this) without proof is still a common mode of human thought.

The Mechanics of Traditional Astrology

L'astrologie hellénistique est l'amalgame d'une doctrine philosophique séduisante, d'une mythologie absurde et des méthodes savantes employées à contre-temps.

[Hellenistic astrology is the amalgam of a seductive philosophical doctrine, an absurd mythology and scientific methods wrongly used.]

A.-J. Festugière, *La Révélation d'Hermès Trismégiste*

As the original aims of certain occult sciences proved arduous or unrealizable, a new strategy was developed: the first goal was scorned and a second, more spiritual goal was put in its place. Unable to make gold, an alchemist could smile mysteriously and confess that he was really practicing an austere kind of yoga. Tarot cards could be made over into vehicles of secret wisdom, having nothing to do with vulgar fortune-telling. The intellectual leaders of astrology now seem to be on the point of giving up prediction altogether and devoting themselves to the music of the spheres. The writings of André Barbault [1] and Dane Rudhyar [2] at their best contain clear echoes of such diverse writers as Blaise Pascal, Carl Jung, and Ralph Waldo Emerson. However, the majority of astrologers are just as they have always been: perfectly willing to turn lead into gold and let the spiritual values take care of themselves. We must now look at the realities of astrological practice, the groundwork of the more mystical structures.

HOROSCOPES

Astrology begins with the natal (birth) horoscope: a geocentric map of the astrological situation at the moment the subject literally or metaphorically emerged from the womb. The subject may be a man, a gorilla, a nation, or an event. The position of the sun, moon, and planets with respect to the zodiac and to one another is of major importance.

The astrological situation is not the same thing as the astronomical situation, although in the early days of astrology it was. For example, astrologically Truman Capote is a Libran with Venus and Neptune in Leo, but on September 30, 1924, when he was born, the sun was in fact in Virgo while Venus and Neptune were in Cancer. This change is caused by the precession of the equinoxes, which is discussed later.

Few modern astrologers spend much time searching out the planets in the night sky. They use astrological tables which refer to the position of the zodiac constellations 2,000 years ago, not to the present reality. Some astrologers find this situation disturbing and are trying to reform it. Others hardly consider it worth mentioning. Still others do not yet know about it.

Astrological tables may be a few millennia off, but they are used carefully and objectively. Most astrologers will produce identical horoscopes for the same time and place.

PRELUDE TO SCIENCE

PLANETS

The ancients called the heavenly bodies that seemed to move among the constellations πλάνητες ἀστέρες (*planētes asteres*), "wandering stars." Their astrological roles are based on their mythological associations.

Sun	☉	Power, masculinity, self-expression
Moon	☽	Fertility, femininity, intuition
Mercury	☿	Intellect, communication, mobility
Venus	♀	Love, emotion, harmony
Mars	♂	Energy, courage, combativeness
Jupiter	♃	Expansiveness, wealth, authority
Saturn	♄	Inhibition, caution, old age

The discovery of three additional planets—Uranus (1781), Neptune (1846), and Pluto (1930)—surprised the astrologers, but with extraordinary pliability they worked each of them into the traditional scheme. They detected in the new planets the very qualities suggested by the names given to them by astronomers:

Uranus	♅	Change, inventiveness, revolution
Neptune	♆	Mysticism, vagueness, fantasy
Pluto	♇	Hidden power, regeneration, transmutation

SIGNS OF THE ZODIAC

The actual zodiac constellations vary in size, so for convenience they were arbitrarily made equal early in the history of astrology. The diagram shows the boundaries of the constellations as seen in the northern hemisphere in the spring. (Sagittarius and

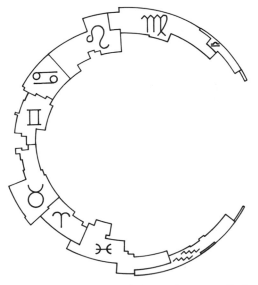

The actual boundaries of the zodiac constellations

parts of Capricorn and Scorpio are not shown, because they are in the southern hemisphere at this time.) The standardized signs of the zodiac as shown in the diagram on page 47 are twelve arcs of 30 degrees each. The system was further standardized by having the spring equinox begin the yearly cycle with the sun at 0 degrees Aries. The sun then moves roughly 1 degree a day until it has "traveled through" all twelve signs.

DEGREES	SIGNS	STARTING DATES
0–30	♈ Aries	March 21
30–60	♉ Taurus	April 21
60–90	♊ Gemini	May 22
90–120	♋ Cancer	June 22
120–150	♌ Leo	July 23
150–180	♍ Virgo	August 24
180–210	♎ Libra	September 24
210–240	♏ Scorpio	October 24

240–270	♐	Sagittarius	November 23
270–300	♑	Capricorn	December 22
300–330	♒	Aquarius	January 21
330–360	♓	Pisces	February 20

The location of the sun at a person's birth usually determines his "sign," but if the sun is the only planet in that sign, he may be placed in another one. Born August 22, 1862, Claude Debussy is technically a Leo. But French astrologers usually consider Debussy, composer of *La Mer* and *Clair de Lune*, as a Cancer—a water sign ruled by the moon. On the other hand, Louis XIV, the Sun King, has been made an honorary Leo—a fire sign ruled by the sun—although technically he is a Virgo (he was born September 5, 1638). Obviously hindsight was a factor in these decisions. Astrological data permit more than one interpretation.

The zodiacal signs are divided into *triplicities* by the four Aristotelian elements: earth, air, fire, and water. The signs in each of these groups form "favorable" angles with one another, so they are considered harmonious and temperamentally similar:

Fire	energetic (choleric)
Air	mentally active (sanguine)
Water	emotional (phlegmatic)
Earth	practical (melancholic)

The signs are also divided into *quadriplicities*, according to whether they begin, typify, or end one of the four seasons. Here the signs in each group form "unfavorable" angles with one another. The cardinal signs are active and enterprising, but these qualities are expressed differently through fire (Aries), water (Cancer), air (Libra), and earth (Capricorn). There is a similar fourfold difference among the fixed signs (firm and intense) and the mutable signs (variable and quick).

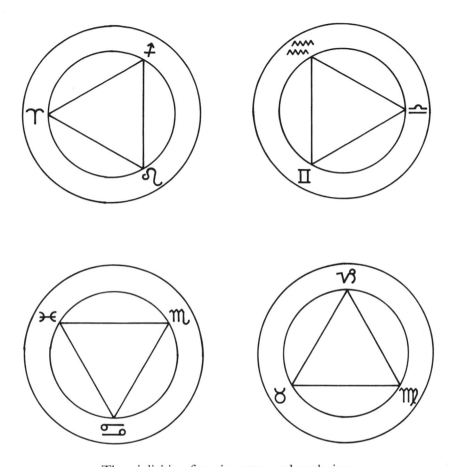

The triplicities: fire, air, water, and earth signs

Each sign of the zodiac is ruled by a planet, or sometimes by two.

SIGN	PLANET	SIGN	PLANET
Aries	Mars	Libra	Venus
Taurus	Venus	Scorpio	Mars (Pluto)
Gemini	Mercury	Sagittarius	Jupiter
Cancer	Moon	Capricorn	Saturn
Leo	Sun	Aquarius	Saturn (Uranus)
Virgo	Mercury	Pisces	Jupiter (Neptune)

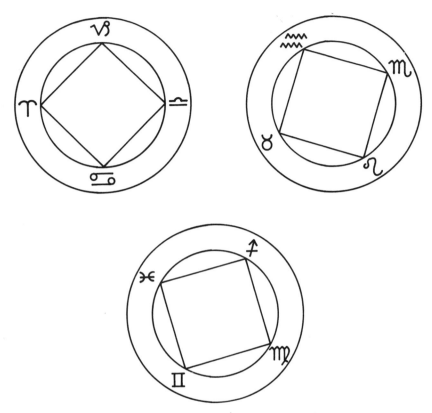

The quadruplicities: cardinal, fixed, and mutable signs

Each planet is at home in its own sign and has affinities with certain other signs but is damaging in certain uncongenial signs. As one might expect, Venus is out of place in Virgo (Goethe), just as Mars is out of place in Cancer (Karl Marx). The moon is out of place in Scorpio (Hector Berlioz) and in Capricorn (Napoleon and Hitler).

Descriptions, crude or subtle, of the character attached to each sign can be found at any newsstand. Universal traits abound, and for anyone dissatisfied with his sign, there are alternatives.

ASCENDANTS

Because of the earth's rotation, each sign of the zodiac seems to pass by overhead every twenty-four hours. The sign that was rising on the eastern horizon at the moment of a person's birth is called his *ascendant* and is considered highly significant. People born at sunrise have the same sun signs and ascendant signs; the sun is "in" the sign that is rising on the eastern horizon. Charles Manson, born at 6:30 a.m. November 12, 1934, is thus a "double Scorpio": at his birth Scorpio was rising (ascendant sign) and the sun was "in" Scorpio (sun sign). But most people have differing sun signs and ascendant signs.

The sun-sign traditionally represents an individual's inner character, while the ascendant represents his outer personality. In practice, the ascendant is a marvelous fudge-factor (one of many in astrology), which permits people who do not like their sun-signs to assume a more congenial identity.

When the ascendant is known, it is placed on the eastern horizon of the horoscope, which now becomes a crude map of the heavens at the moment of birth. The actor Charles Chaplin was born at 8:00 p.m. on April 16, 1889. The conventional form of his horoscope shown in diagram *a* on page 58 can be translated directly into a three-dimensional geocentric map (diagram *b*). The sun had set below the western horizon; the moon was just rising in the east. Except for Mercury and Jupiter, the planets were visible overhead in the night sky. The constellation Scorpio, Chaplin's ascendant, had risen 9 degrees in the east.

HOUSES

This touchy subject finds astrologers in profound disarray. The original idea was simple enough: the celestial sphere around the

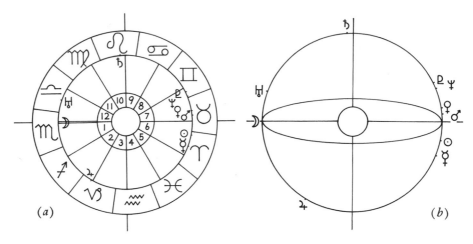

Charles Chaplin's horoscope: (*a*) conventional form; (*b*) as a geocentric planetary map

earth was arbitrarily divided, starting at the eastern horizon, into twelve houses, each corresponding to some area of human life:

1	Self, appearance
2	Possessions, loss and gain
3	Communication
4	Home
5	Pleasure, love affairs
6	Health, well-being
7	Partners, marriage
8	Death, legacies
9	Philosophy, travel
10	Career, status
11	Friends
12	Restraints

The positions of the houses are fixed, so how they are filled—with which planets and signs—is determined by the ascendant. Interpretive possibilities are far more interesting and varied when the ascendant is known. Napoleon was born at 11:00 a.m. August 15, 1769, when Scorpio was the ascendant (diagram *a*). If the hour

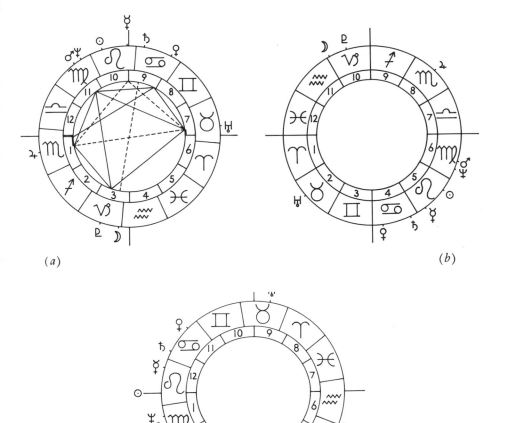

Napoleon's horoscope: (*a*) Scorpio ascendant; (*b*) no ascendant, "standard" form; (*c*) no ascendant, "solar" form

of birth and consequently the ascendant had not been known, the data could have been presented in one of three other ways. The first is by placing the houses and the signs in the "standard" position, Aries coinciding with House 1 on the eastern horizon (diagram *b*). In the second method the signs are rotated to place the sun on the eastern horizon, producing a "solar chart" (diagram *c*). The third way is by "rectifying" the horoscope, which means that the astrologer simply guesses what the ascendant was on the basis of his intuition and the known facts of the subject's life.

The question of how to divide the houses has been bitterly debated for centuries and is still unresolved. To begin with, the houses were marked off equally on the ecliptic. But more sophisticated mathematical methods were later introduced by Campanus (thirteenth century), Regiomontanus (fifteenth century), and Placidus (seventeenth century), and each has attracted followers. There are now more than half a dozen rival systems. The Placidean system is the most widely used today, partly because Placidean tables have long been the most easily obtainable. However, there is a growing trend toward returning to the Equal House method.

The differences among the systems are minor in southern Europe and the United States. Napoleon's horoscope (Ajaccio, Corsica, latitude 42 degrees) is virtually the same in the Placidean and Equal House systems. Farther north, however, the Placidean system becomes increasingly distorted. In Tchaikowsky's horoscope (Votkinsk, Russia, latitude 58 degrees), the two methods place the planets in different houses (diagrams *a* and *b*). Obviously the interpretations of the two charts will be different.

In the Equal House chart the moon is in the First House (ego), while in the Placidean chart the moon is in the Second House (money): the first shows an individual with a sensitive, introspective character, while the second shows an individual sensitive and concerned about money.

In the Equal House chart Neptune is in the Eighth House (death): an individual with unorthodox and secretive ideas about death and sex. In the Placidean chart Neptune is in the Ninth House (travel): an individual who may get lost while traveling.

In the Equal House chart both the Tenth House (career) and

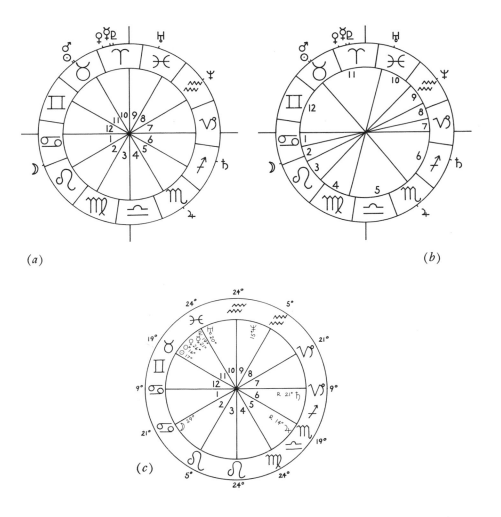

Tchaikowsky's horoscope: (*a*) Equal House System; (*b*) European Placidean system; (*c*) English Placidean system

the Eleventh House (friends) are strong. In the Placidean chart the Tenth House is empty except for Uranus, while the Eleventh House is occupied by five planets: this suggests an individual who achieves little in his career and devotes all his energies to socializing.

A talented astrologer can give a plausible interpretation for nearly any horoscope, but considering the facts of Tchaikowsky's life, the Equal House chart seems to supply the more promising raw material.

Nevertheless, many respected astrologers continue to use the Placidean method, so a serious student of astrology is forced to learn it—as Baudelaire learned English in order to read Poe. European Placideans like André Barbault show the actual size of the houses and keep the zodiac signs equal; in this way, the aspects can be shown with their correct angular value (diagram *b*). English and American Placideans, however, present the houses as equal and compress or expand the zodiac signs to fit them; the true state of affairs is indicated by the angles written at twelve points around the periphery (diagram *c*).

ASPECTS

The angles the planets make with one another as seen from earth are considered "easy," "favorable," and "harmonious" or the reverse, in varying degrees. The major aspects are given in the table.

NAME	ANGLE (DEGREES)	SYMBOL	DESCRIPTION
Conjunction	0	☌	Strong (effects depend on planets involved)
Sextile	60	✳	Fairly strong, favorable
Square	90	☐	Strong, unfavorable
Trine	120	△	Strong, favorable
Opposition	180	☍	Strong, unfavorable

Beginners can see how planets "in opposition" to each other might be called unfavorable, but not why 60 degrees should be favorable and 90 degrees unfavorable.

The answer lies in numerology, the mystic numerology of Pythagoras (c. 582–500 B.C.) and his school at Crotona in southern Italy. Aspects give defenders of astrology a great deal of trouble.

PROGRESSIONS AND TRANSITS

If character is destiny, the horoscope is already a start in predicting the future. For more detailed and specific predictions, however, additional calculations can be made.

The simplest and most illogical is the "progressed horoscope." If a client wants to know what will happen in his fiftieth year, a horoscope for a date fifty days after his birthday is plotted. (An error of four minutes will throw the prediction off by twelve months.) If the client was born September 1, 1940, the horoscope for October 21, 1940, is plotted and presumed to represent the client's life in 1990. No reason has ever been advanced for this procedure, except that "it works." It may be that in skilled hands any horoscope works.

A second method, which at least pays some attention to astronomical reality, is the study of "transits." The planetary situation at the time being considered is plotted and then superimposed on the client's natal horoscope. The new relationships and aspects so formed are studied.

INTERPRETATION

The basic working materials of astrology have now been presented. Most of them would have been perfectly familiar to Claudius Ptolemy eighteen centuries ago. The critical factor is the way they are used, the amount of skill and intuition displayed by the astrologer in his interpretation.

It is often suggested that divination methods do little more than furnish props for a gifted person: to focus his attention, to set his special talents in motion, to permit him to express hunches and shrewd guesses. If so, people who are trying to make astrology "scientific" have missed the point.

The critical role played by interpretation in astrology can be seen by comparing the horoscopes of two Leos, born a day apart, the times not known, so each horoscope is presented as a solar chart. One belonged to the writer Aldous Huxley, the other to the actor Walter Brennan. Except for the position of the moon, the horoscopes are nearly identical. Yet an accomplished astrologer could produce two highly differentiated character analyses from this material. First of all, he could "rectify" the horoscopes by giving each a different ascendant. Then he could contrast the moon in Aries (quick-tempered) with the moon in Taurus (love for the good

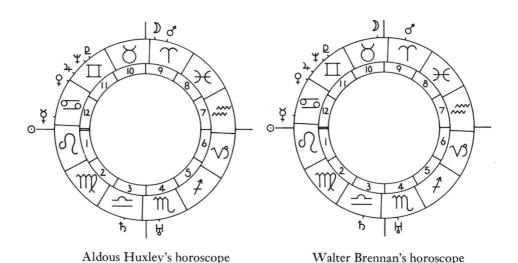

Aldous Huxley's horoscope   Walter Brennan's horoscope

things of life). From these two differences, he could construct two different sets of aspects. Each of the resulting interpretations would bear a recognizable and perhaps even striking resemblance to its subject.

In most horoscopes the astrological data are usually abundant and contradictory, so that the range of possibilities for selection, emphasis, and interpretation is very great indeed. This may be what keeps astrology viable.

SEVEN

Making Astrology "Scientific"

Astrology isn't a science, it's a disease.
Maimonides, *Responsa I*

It is perhaps just this irrationalism, this intuitive and
mysterious basis of astrology, that is (and has always been)
the sole source of its appeal—and one of the main reasons
why scientific investigations of astrology seem to lack
appeal even for astrologers.
Louis MacNeice, *Astrology*

Like the arts and the humanities, astrology has watched the rise
of science and felt certain pressures to reform itself, or at
least to adopt protective coloration of a scientific nature.
Defenders of astrology usually take one of three positions toward
it:

(1) Science itself is shot through with irrationality, its premises are
indefensible, and anyway scientists are a rather shabby lot so
who cares what they think?

(2) Being irrational is what gives astrology its value; therefore trying to make it scientific will only spoil it.

(3) Astrology today exists in a degenerate form, but if a tough

scientific line is followed, with rigorous statistical analyses, objective experimentation, and sweeping reforms, astrology will take its rightful place as one of the sciences.

Science is repudiated altogether in the first two positions, so only the last concerns us here. Publications with such titles as *The Scientific Basis of Astrology*, "Astrology Faces Modern Thought," *Astrology: Science or Superstition?*, and *The Case for Astrology* are currently available. Does this trend mean that astrology will soon be accepted as a science, or perhaps already is a science unfairly snubbed by Establishment science? What are the most serious objections to astrology from a scientific point of view?

THE SHIFTING ZODIAC

The idea of being able to locate oneself by means of the stars is an attractive one. In the twentieth century it is rare to find someone who can tell whether the moon is waxing or waning, let alone identify a constellation. Perhaps astrology is a way of rediscovering one's place in the cosmos. Could one become so familiar with the heavens through astrology that if dropped into a wilderness one could instantly determine time, place, season, and compass points?

Alas, no. Few astrologers spend any time looking at the sky. For centuries astrology has been an indoors, bookish operation, basing its calculations on tables long detached from astronomical reality.

You may read in an astrological table that Mars entered Taurus on Christmas Day, 1973, but if you had happened to step outside and look that night, you would have seen Mars in the constellation Aries, where it remained for the next two months. In the same way, a natal horoscope is not a real picture of the heavens at the moment of one's birth; most of the Scorpios of this world were really born when the sun was in Libra, most Leos are really Cancers, Cancers are Geminis, and so on.

Claudius Ptolemy tied the signs of the zodiac to the τροπαί, or turning points, in the second century A.D., creating the "tropical zodiac":

0°	Aries	spring equinox
0°	Cancer	summer solstice
0°	Libra	fall equinox
0°	Capricorn	winter solstice

At that time the sun actually did enter Aries at the spring equinox, and it was a great convenience to have the calculations of all the astrologers of the ancient world standardized in this way. It was such a convenience, in fact, that it was clung to even after it ceased to be accurate.

Because the earth is flattened at the poles and subject to attractive forces from other parts of the solar system, it gradually turns around the pole of the ecliptic, so that the equinoxes advance 50 minutes each year, or 1 degree in 72 years. The complete 360-degree cycle takes almost 26,000 years. This is the "precession of the equinoxes," and as a result of it the spring equinox has gradually slipped backward through the zodiac. It has passed through nearly all 30 degrees of Pisces and is now approaching Aquarius. Since the real Pisces and Aquarius overlap, it is hard to tell exactly where one ends and the other begins, unless one accepts the 30-degree standard length for all zodiac constellations. This is why there are so many opinions about when the Age of Aquarius started or will start.

Astrology thus orients its followers not to today's cosmos, but to the cosmos of the second century A.D. According to Gibbon, that was a glorious moment in world history, "the Golden Age of Trajan and the Antonines," when mankind was most happy and prosperous. Astrology might be looked upon as a charming memorial to that period.

Most astrologers either do not know about equinoctial precession or claim that it does not matter. A few, however, are trying to make reforms. They are called "sidereal astrologers" (*sidereus*, starry, celestial), since they want to abandon the tropical zodiac and use the present sidereal or actual zodiac. They are generally condemned or ignored.

"At the moment, in England and America, there is a small but noisy contingent of astrologers who contend . . . that *only* the moving Sidereal zodiac is the true one, and they have tried to buttress their argument with elaborate statistical studies. Their opponents (the majority of conventional astrologers) contend that the statistics can be interpreted in a number of ways, and insist that their own collective experience testifies to the validity of the standard Tropical zodiac." [1]

The American astrologer Marc Edmund Jones maintains that the zodiac constellations "are seldom used in astrology"; [2] they are merely a learning device, "entirely artificial, of course, but it can be exceedingly useful if not permitted to become more than an aid to the eye, or a mental construct to help the imaginative faculties." [3] A reformer in his own right, Jones has tried for years to induce astrologers to correct their pronunciation of Pisces from PIEseeze to PISSeeze, without success.

Dane Rudhyar, a disciple of Jones, dismisses sidereal astrology because "I do not believe that this type of astrology is what we need today—that is, it does not fill *the psychological need* of our present humanity." [4]

The siderealist position is fully developed by the English astrologer Rupert Gleadow in *The Zodiac Revealed*.[5] In his system the zodiac signs begin on the following dates, which are close to the times when the sun does in fact enter each constellation:

Aries	April 13
Taurus	May 14
Gemini	June 13
Cancer	July 15
Leo	August 16
Virgo	September 16
Libra	October 16
Scorpio	November 16
Sagittarius	December 15
Capricorn	January 14
Aquarius	February 12
Pisces	March 14

This causes some startling changes. Mozart, long admired as the perfect Aquarian composer, is changed into a Capricorn. Stalin and Nixon (Capricorn) become jolly Sagittarians. Pablo Picasso (Scorpio) becomes a winsome Libran, while Grandma Moses (Virgo) becomes a roistering Leo. Former Gemini composers Edward Elgar and Richard Strauss now join Liberace in Taurus.

All of this is upsetting to a traditionally oriented astrologer, which helps to explain the negative reaction the siderealists have received. No scientific objections have been raised so far—just appeals to tradition, habit, and "need," mixed with sarcasm and emotional non sequiturs. The protests were shriller when in 1970 Steven Schmidt published *Astrology 14: Your New Sun Sign.*[6] Schmidt not only made Pisces instead of Aries begin on the spring equinox, he added two new constellations to the zodiac.

In Figure 1 of his book, he points out, "there are not only the traditional 12 signs occupying the belt of the zodiac—there are 14!" Cetus the Whale and Ophiuchus the Serpent-Slayer are outside the zodiac, both in the sky and in his Figure 1, but that does not faze him. He puts Cetus between Aries and Taurus, Ophiuchus between Scorpio and Sagittarius.

The characters of the two new signs are sketchily defined. In Cetus the Whale ("extremely charming, though headstrong") we find Dame Margot Fonteyn, Bob Dylan, and Sir Laurence Olivier. Ophiuchians are also charming, with a great need "to express their sensitivity and talent." Noel Coward, Dorothy Lamour, and Woodrow Wilson are some of the strange bedfellows in this sign.

Libra is traditionally the sign for charm in the zodiac. Astrology 14 provides three charm signs, which may be more than the system can carry. Not the least of Astrology 14's problems is the number fourteen itself. Twelve is charged with mythological and religious associations and is numerologically heavy as well. But fourteen is notably lacking in charisma.

If the stars are held to influence human destiny, it would certainly be helpful if astrological tables showed their actual locations. To claim that star position does not matter merely adds to the confusion, since it obviously did matter to the ancients. At what time did it stop mattering, and why? If the position of the stars does not matter, why use the word "astrology"?

UNTESTED PREMISES

What makes scientists especially nervous about astrology is that the entire structure as outlined in chapter 6 is based on claims and assumptions that no one has tested:

that there are twelve basic types of human character;
that one's character is determined by the time of year in which one
    was born;
that one's life is controlled or influenced by ten of the 5,000 visible
    heavenly bodies;
and so on.

PRELUDE TO SCIENCE

Astrology works backwards. It begins with a highly detailed conclusion, then forces as many facts as possible to fit it, discarding the rest. A few examples show how deep the gulf is between this attitude and science.

Personality Traits and the Zodiac. The American physician and psychologist William H. Sheldon devoted years of research at Harvard to studying all varieties of human body shape and the personality traits associated with each. After careful statistical analyses of the correlations, he presented his three basic personality types, each with twenty specific individual traits.[7] Not everyone agrees with his conclusions, but the process by which he reached them was undeniably scientific and is open to critical review.

The twelve zodiac types evolved somewhat differently. The constellations were named and established first. When personality traits were assigned to go with them, these were derived from the constellations themselves rather than from individuals. People born under Taurus are solid, stubborn, possessive, thick-set—bull-like, in other words. Leos are proud, dignified, strong, "born leaders"—in short, leonine. Scorpios are secretive and revengeful. Virgos are compulsively neat. . . .

If each of the signs is summarized with a single adjective, one obtains:

♈	Assertive	♎	Harmonious
♉	Possessive	♏	Passionate
♊	Changeable	♐	Expansive
♋	Sensitive	♑	Prudent
♌	Creative	♒	Detached
♍	Critical	♓	Intuitive

Nearly everyone in the world will behave in each of these ways many times in the course of a year. Whatever a person's sign happens to be, it will most likely emphasize, usually in a flattering way, a trait he already possesses. This means that the zodiac signs are not very useful taxonomically; they do not provide a way of classifying human nature into distinctive mutually exclusive groups; the traits are too general, too widely shared.

However, the zodiac is not used to classify various human temperaments as they manifest themselves in daily life. The signs are allotted to individuals according to the time of birth, before the temperament has developed. Obviously it is not science to announce the conclusion before the experiment has been run.

The more widely shared the traits of the zodiac types happen to be, the less likelihood of glaring discrepancies between an individual's actual personality and his assigned zodiac personality, and the less chance of astrology's ever being proved wrong. But theories so framed that they can never be proved wrong are not science.

Attributes of the Planets. The ancients named the planets after gods by simple analogy: a reddish planet was the war god Mars, a quick-moving planet was the messenger god Mercury, the slowest planet was the aged Saturn. Later, astrological influences were attributed to them not by experimentation but by their names: Venus must bring love, Saturn must bring old age, Mars must bring injury and bad news, and so on.

Once again, conclusions were drawn and applied arbitrarily. But of course most people actually do love and grow old and receive good and bad news.

The process was repeated as astronomers discovered and named the three new planets. By the most extraordinary coincidence, astrologers concluded, these names furnished the key to their astrological characters. Thanks to Freud, Uranus is remembered chiefly as having been castrated by his son, but before that he had sired monsters and led a turbulent life. Astrologers made the planet Uranus a bringer of change and disruption and held it responsible for the Industrial Revolution. They gave Neptune a watery, mystical character and put it in charge of Pisces. They made Pluto ruler of all underground activities and the subconscious.

The Houses. Each of the twelve divisions of the celestial sphere determined by the individual's ascendant represents some area of human activity. But why should one of these vast segments of space govern one person's love affairs, another person's death, and still another's tendency to take long trips? On what evidence was the assumption made?

The Aspects. Astrology states that when two planets shine on a newborn baby at an angle of 90 degrees, the effect is damaging, but the same planets shining at an angle of 120 degrees are beneficial. Why this should be so is not explained. Neither is how the rays of Venus and the moon combine so that at a favorable angle they make a person vivacious and inspired like Jean-Paul Sartre and Sir Laurence Olivier and at an unfavorable angle make another person highstrung and possibly immoral like Oscar Wilde and Sarah Bernhardt.

The subject of aspects raises a still more basic problem: what exactly are the planets emitting which can be so altered by the angles at which they strike?

WHAT IS THE PHYSICAL AGENT?

Roman and Renaissance scholars argued that since the sun controls the seasons by means of radiation, the moon and the planets must also influence human life by means of *radii* (rays). This raises more questions than it answers, however.

With thousands of ray-emitting objects in the sky, why are only the rays from just eight of them (besides the sun and moon) effective on human life? How do these rays differ from all the others? How do they differ from one another, since each planet has a different effect? How are they modified by the zodiac stars (located light-years away), since the effect of each planet must change as it moves from one zodiac sign to another?

The sun, moon, and planets shine on large numbers of people at the same time, yet their effects are supposed to vary according to each person's birth horoscope. How do the rays sense these individual differences? Do the rays permanently alter each individual's cells at birth, so that his response to all future sunshine, moonshine, and starshine is automatically personalized?

If the astrological situation into which an infant is born marks him for life, newborn babies must be extraordinarily sensitive to "rays." But for how long? And in what tissues? If the planetary rays alter an infant's genes, how can the laws of heredity continue to operate?

Astrological influences begin, not at conception, but at the exact moment of birth. Since planetary rays are just as influential below the horizon as above it, they must be able to penetrate up to 8,000 miles of the earth without loss of potency. Why is it that these same rays are unable to penetrate the womb?

Rays with such properties were certainly not known to ancient or medieval apologists, but within the last hundred years remarkable new rays have been discovered. Many occultists hope that "some kind of rays" will one day provide a respectable physical basis for occult phenomena.

All the known electromagnetic rays can be listed according to their wavelengths, from shortest to longest.

TYPE OF RADIATION	WAVELENGTH (METERS)
Cosmic rays	0.000000000000001
Gamma rays	0.0000000000001
X rays	0.0000000001
Ultraviolet light	0.0000001
Visible light	0.000001
Infrared radiation	0.0001
Radio waves	
Radar	0.01
UHF	0.1
VHF	1.0
Short	10.0
Medium and long	1,000.0
Audio frequencies	1,000,000.0

The Scottish physicist James Clerk Maxwell and others showed in the 1860s how electricity and magnetism were related to light waves; two decades later the German physicist Heinrich Hertz began generating radio waves; and by 1901 the Italian inventor Guglielmo Marconi was transmitting radio messages across the Atlantic. Extraterrestrial sources of radio waves were not detected until 1931, when the American radio engineer Karl Jansky noted "cosmic static" coming from the constellation Sagittarius. Radar equipment was used after World War II for picking up short-wave emissions from stars. The sun was found to be continually sending out weak radio waves, with sunspots and solar flares acting as ultra-short-wave transmitters. Venus, Jupiter, and Saturn also emit radio waves.

All this was most encouraging to astrologers. Certain heavenly bodies did in fact "emit rays" which could be detected on earth. The rays themselves proved to be disappointing, however. Nothing from outer space could approach in quantity the radio waves that were being generated all over the earth without noticeably affecting anyone's destiny.

A more powerful kind of radiation from outer space was detected early in the twentieth century. Gases are normally poor conductors of electricity, but when exposed to radiation of sufficient energy the electrons of some gas atoms are knocked loose, forming positively and negatively charged ion pairs. "Ionized" gases do conduct electricity and the extent of the ionization can be easily measured. Materials in the environment emit enough "ionizing radiation" to maintain 500 to 1,000 ions in each cubic centimeter of air.

However, it was noticed that even when containers of pure air or gas were shielded with lead, ionization still occurred. Moreover, the ionization increased when the gas container was elevated in a balloon. (The Austrian physicist Victor Hess was awarded a Nobel Prize in 1936 for demonstrating this fact in 1912.) If the ionization was being caused by radioactive materials on the earth's surface, it would have decreased at higher elevations. But at 9,000 meters the ionization in the gas sample was fifty times greater than at sea level. The implication was strong that penetrating radiation—ten times more penetrating than gamma rays—must be striking the earth from outer space. The term "cosmic rays" was coined by the American physicist Robert A. Millikan in 1926.

The intensity of the cosmic-ray bombardment of earth has not varied for several million years: the distribution of the rays is influenced by the earth's magnetic field. Most cosmic rays originate from the Milky Way galaxy, with the sun contributing some of the lower-energy particles. Sunspots and other signs of solar activity reduce cosmic-ray intensity. The sun completes its rotation every twenty-seven days, and there is a dip in the cosmic-ray intensity at the point where the sunspots confront earth.[8]

Thus the earth receives all manner of waves and radiation, some of it at random, some of it in cycles. Events at a distance—solar activity, for example—do affect conditions on earth.

None of this is very helpful to astrology, however. It is a long way from saying that the heavens emit electromagnetic rays to saying that the heavens control individual destiny. Astrology claims that a very specific set of influences—signs, planets, aspects, houses, transits—are at work, and the new rays are no more able to achieve this than the old ones were.

Lately, the ionized air produced by radiation has been proposed as the physical agent of astrology. Air ions are invisible, "electrical," neatly divided into negative ("good") ions and positive ("bad") ions; the term "ion" itself is austerely scientific, yet reminiscent of the mysterious "bions" of the Austrian psychoanalyst Wilhelm Reich.

Beginning in the 1920s claims were made that negatively ionized air benefited a variety of clinical conditions—asthma, hay fever, depression, high blood pressure. In the late 1950s major electronics firms began marketing ion generators. The *Reader's Digest* published an optimistic article, "Ions Can Do Strange Things to You" (October 1960). For six years I was engaged in research in this area and learned that under special laboratory conditions ionized gases could produce measurable physiological effects on animals and plants, but they were too slight to be of practical use.[9]

Having, like S. J. Perelman, "all of the allergies and none of the talent of Marcel Proust," I tested an ion generator on myself. The one time that I seemed to detect a beneficial effect, I found the apparatus was unplugged.

Today it is startling to see this early research cited as evidence that air ions are important in alchemy (as mentioned earlier), in astrology, in ESP, and in the human environment.[10] Surely something a little stronger is required for all that.

SYNCHRONICITY

The difficulties involved in trying to prove that heavenly bodies act on human destiny must have made Carl Jung's theory of synchronicity (coincidence in time) seem like a godsend.

Jung saw synchronicity as a psychic phenomenon, an irruption from the collective unconscious. At the same time, he hoped to apply ideas of relative truth and noncausal events from particle physics to human affairs, particularly to telepathy and clairvoyance. However, even though he had the distinguished physicist Wolfgang Pauli as an adviser, his exposition is far from clear.

Jung calls synchronicity "an acausal connecting principle" and describes it as a meaningful coincidence of two or more events not causally connected but related in significance. If valid, it would free astrology from the struggle to prove causality. It applies only when the two events "are not connected by the same acting cause." [11]

Meaningful coincidences are real enough, but by invoking synchronicity one seems to be merely substituting one mystery for another. Research workers are often surprised by how quickly they can think up plausible theories for data that later turns out to be incorrect. In the same way, a person's psychological predispositions can make any coincidence meaningful, just as they can make Rorschach blots meaningful.

Has anything been discovered or explained by using the term synchronicity? Jahoda calls it "a mere verbal label serving as a pseudo-explanation" and emphasizes that it is a universal human trait to find meanings for every sequence of events.[12]

Yet synchronicity still commands interest, both as a collaborative effort by a psychologist and a physicist (although Pauli's contribution seems to have been minor) and as an attempt to break out of conventional thought patterns. The principle of acausality was not stated very well by Jung, but someone else may state it better.

EIGHT

Has Astrology Value?

Basically astrology's a lot of stuff to make people happy.
The Question Man, *San Francisco Chronicle*,
30 August 1972

The title of this chapter tends to bring latent scientism to the surface: "How can astrology possibly have any value when it is not scientific?" A devastating question, if one assumes that only science has value.

Few astrologers have ever seriously claimed that astrology is a science. Most of its followers don't care whether it is or not. Even a religious thinker as sly and original as the late Alan Watts described astrology as "a primitive science which is correct in theory but inexact and unworkable in practice" [1] (correct, that is to say, insofar as it recognizes that one's life is influenced by the here and now). After reviewing the evidence of the last chapter, one can reasonably say that astrology has no value *as science*. But there are other grounds for valuing, or despising, astrology.

One of the most serious charges against it is that it denies free will and that like organized religion it may be used to drug or distract the masses. The Jewish philosopher Maimonides (1135–1204) leveled his attacks specifically against predestination, the idea that the stars controlled destiny and therefore it was a waste of time for man to use his reason and order his life. Even so, the common Yiddish phrase *"mazel tov"* (congratulations for good luck) means "may your planetary influences be favorable"; *mazel* originally referred to a planet.[2] Horoscopes were routinely drawn up for children in the Middle Ages; no doubt many waited complacently all their lives for the predicted goodies to materialize.

In an article first published in the *Daily Worker* in the 1930s, the English biologist J. B. S. Haldane sharply attacked astrology's predictive ability:

"If the astrologers and palmists want to convince scientists of the truth of their 'sciences,' they have an easy task. No doubt (if their claims are right) they must have discovered that millions of young men were going to die between 1914 and 1918. So they ought to be able to predict the dates of future wars. When they get a few such dates right I shall take them seriously. But I am not much impressed by a few lucky shots."

He went on to voice the familiar socialist objections: "However that may be, astrologers and palmists are very useful to the cause of capitalism. They help to persuade people that their destinies are outside their control. And, of course, this is true as long as enough people believe it. But if enough people learn how the joint fate of us all can be altered, things begin to happen which mean the end of capitalism as well as of astrology and palmistry."[3]

Aldous Huxley made a still more devastating attack on astrology in his novel *Crome Yellow:*

" 'You find me busy at my horoscopes,' she said. . . . Most of Priscilla's days were spent in casting the horoscopes of horses, and she invested her money scientifically, as the Stars dictated. She betted on football too, and had a large notebook in which she registered the horoscopes of all the players in all the teams of the League. The process of balancing the horoscopes of two elevens one against the other was a very delicate and difficult one. A match between the Spurs and the Villa entailed a conflict in the heavens so vast and so complicated that it was not to be wondered at if she sometimes made a mistake about the outcome." [4]

Astrologers retreat from untenable positions, however. They now maintain that "the stars impel, but do not compel" and that "astrological prophecy is unreliable and no sensible astrologer would maintain otherwise." [5] Some astrologers are able to have it both ways; they scorn predictions, yet at the same time insist that they *could* predict if they wanted to and narrate endless cases in which it was done successfully.

Sometimes astrology is attacked on moral grounds, because "it isn't true." Even truth can be used destructively, however. Truth as a weapon in the hands of ignorant or unbalanced persons has been thoroughly explored in such classic dramas as Ibsen's *The Wild Duck* and Eugene O'Neill's *The Iceman Cometh*. The danger arises when a limited truth is maintained at the expense of a larger one.

On the positive side, astrology has always been used as a kind of crude, do-it-yourself psychotherapy. It gives people an excuse for thinking about themselves for hours at a time. Whatever their sign, they can compare what it says about them with what their friends say about them and what they think about themselves. In a society that denies ego support to most people, astrology provides it at a very low price.

As it is now practiced, astrology will not help a person get "back to nature." But people who go on to do a little stargazing on their own often do get there eventually. Even if astrology does not instantly connect its followers with the universe, it does connect them with other people. So many people have thought about astrology for so long, that a kind of accumulated energy fills its admittedly irrational system and gives support, social and psychic.

Some people use astrology as a game. The pleasures of recreation may not be the highest in the world, but they are undeniably real pleasures.

Finally, astrology has been and remains a rich source of raw material for the arts—painting, classical music, rock, ballet, and literature. What André Barbault builds from the common materials of astrology is comparable to what Greek playwrights made out of common legends.

NINE

The Kabbalah: Letters and Numbers of Power

```
A B R A C A D A B R A
A B R A C A D A B R
A B R A C A D A B
A B R A C A D A
A B R A C A D
A B R A C A
A B R A C
A B R A
A B R
A B
A
```

(Traditional kabbalistic talisman)

Within this circle is Jehovah's name
Forward and backward anagrammatized . . .
Then fear not, Faustus, to be resolute
And try the utmost magic can perform.
Christopher Marlowe, *Doctor Faustus*

Nearly every religion has a body of secret traditions which is transmitted only to its most elite and devout members. The Hebrew mystical tradition known as the Kabbalah (קַבָּלָה, *qabbalah*, received lore, commonly spelled "cabala" in English), is a special case in that during the Renaissance it was appropriated by Christian mystics and made to play a variety of roles quite divorced from its origins.

The earliest kabbalist document is the *Sefer Yezira* (*Book of Creation*), written by a Jewish neo-Pythagorean in one of the "Babylonian" yeshivas, probably in the third century (although the tradition of "secret meanings" to be found in the Hebrew text of Genesis, Ezekiel, and other books of the Bible is certainly much older). Considered to be divinely inspired, the *Yezira* describes how God used the twenty-two letters of the Hebrew alphabet to create the world. Unique powers are said to remain in these letters, especially in the four letters making up the name of God (the tetragrammaton). The *Yezira* was brought to Jews in Italy in the ninth century A.D.; then it spread to Germany, southern France, and Spain. Three centuries later the *Sefer ha Bahir* (*Book of Light*), a mystical commentary on the first chapter of Genesis, was compiled, probably in southern France. Toward the end of the thirteenth century the *Sefer ha Zohar* (*Book of Splendor*) was published by Moses ben Shem Tob in Spain.

Of the three kabbalist classics, the most popular has been the *Zohar:* a mind-boggling compendium of prayers, spells, biblical numerology, folktales, methods of divination, exorcism, and ways of obtaining Hidden Power and Secret Wisdom.[1]

Many influences have been detected in the kabbalist writings —Pythagorean numerology, Zoroastrianism, neo-Platonism, the Gnostic teachings of Syria and Egypt, the Apocryphal writings excluded from the Hebrew and Christian Scriptures. Poverty and isolation—intellectual energy deprived of normal outlets—surely played a part in its development. For medieval Jews it must have offered a thrilling alternative to the rationalism of Maimonides and the pedantry of Talmudic scholars. The Hasidic movement embraced it enthusiastically. In times of political terror, it created a favorable climate for ecstatic evangelism and "false Messiahs" like Sabbatai Zevi (1626–1676).

The Kabbalah: Letters and Numbers of Power

One of the most characteristic preoccupations of the kabbalists is *gematria*, the use of the numerical values of the letters in the Hebrew alphabet to discover new meanings in scriptural words and passages. Anagrams were made of individual words, or new words were systematically built out of the old words by substituting letters in accordance with secret alphabets, a technique known as *temurah*. The meaning of a single word could be expanded through *notaricon*, in which each letter was considered to be the first letter of another word, so that single words could give rise to whole sentences. In these ways, new meanings could be derived endlessly from the scriptures.

· The Unutterable Name of God consists of four letters: *yodh* (י), *he* (ה), *vau* (ו), and *he* (ה), written from right to left as יהוה. The numerical values of these letters (10, 5, 6, and 5) add up to 26. Since the word for unity is אחד (1 + 8 + 4) and the word for love is אהבה (1 + 5 + 2 + 5), both totaling 13, one can say that Love is Unity and that God is Unity manifested as Love.

Since all twenty-two Hebrew letters are consonants, vowels must be indicated by small dots or symbols above and below the letters. YHVH was never to be pronounced: the word *adonai* was usually spoken in its place. As a reminder, the vowel markings for *adonai* were added to YHVH. When a papal scribe translating a Hebrew text into Latin in 1516 incorrectly applied these vowel sounds to YHVH, the non-word "Jehovah" was created.

Cultural exchange in the Renaissance did not consist entirely of study by Europeans of the works of dead Greeks and Romans. Christian intellectuals also studied Hebrew. More and more Jews printed and published books, made translations, taught at universities. From this time on, the Kabbalah exercised an irresistible fascination on Christian occultists. Magicians used kabbalist formulas to dress up their rituals. Zealots twisted the Kabbalah into smarmy tracts designed to convert the Jews. "Adam Kadmon," described in the *Zohar* as the highest manifestation of God, was equated by pious Christians with Jesus Christ. Rosicrucianism, freemasonry, and many other secret societies borrowed freely from the Kabbalah.

Rightly or wrongly understood, the Kabbalah influenced many major figures of the Renaissance and the "hermetic" sixteenth century: the Italian humanist Giovanni Pico della Mirandola (1463–1494), the French seer Nostradamus (1503–1566), the German occultist Cornelius Agrippa (1486?–1535), the English scholar Robert Fludd (1574–1637). Even the great Dutch philosopher Baruch Spinoza (1632–1677) has been accused by a kabbalist scholar (quoted by the American Rabbi Herbert Weiner) of cribbing from the *Zohar*.

Some of these figures seem to have had a genuine understanding of the Kabbalah; others bent and distorted it, occasionally producing works of monumental silliness. The process is by no means complete today.

The Tree of Life, or "tree of the *sefirot*," has passed into general occult usage. Since one of the names of God is *Ein Sof* (The Infinite One), his ten divine manifestations are called *sefirot* (singular, *sefira*). Arranged as a tree of ten spheres connected by twenty-two paths, these symbolize a descent from the godhead to earth—the pattern of creation and also the source of *shefa*, divine grace. Conversely, the Tree of Life is a map showing how the soul can work its way up again, sphere by sphere, to union with God.

While it is convenient to represent them as a tree, the *sefirot* are not so much isolated way stations as they are spheres within spheres. Creation begins as a pure emanation from God (*Kether*) and acquires successive layers until it achieves physical reality (*Malkuth*). In the case of man, the outermost layer is the body; at death, the physical body is discarded, followed by the other layers as the soul ascends to God.

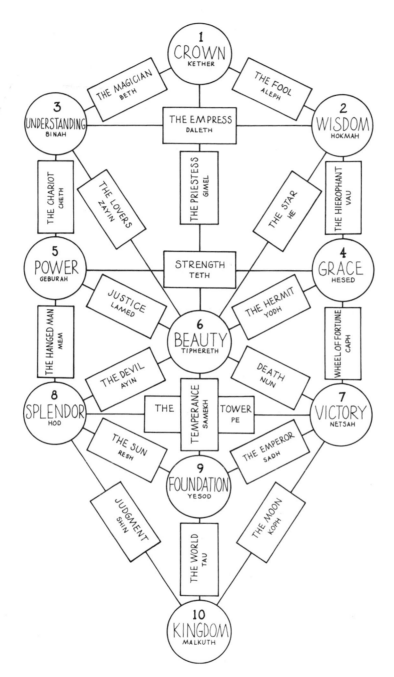

The Tree of Life, showing the ten *sefirot* and the twenty-two paths, with
Tarot correspondences after Aleister Crowley

(89)

This basically simple scheme is capable of endless refinements. Abstract sexual elements, analogous to the Chinese yin/yang principle and the *chakras* of tantric yoga, have been incorporated into it. The *sefirot* on the left side of the tree (3, 5, 8) are female, while those on the right side (2, 4, 7) are male. The first triangle (1, 2, 3) represents the primal creative activity of God, the intellectual world, and in literal terms the head. The second triangle (4, 5, 6) represents evolving life, organization, the arms and trunk. The third triangle (7, 8, 9) is the physical world, the legs and genitals. *Malkuth* (10) represents earth and includes all the other *sefirot*.

Various occult groups such as the Hermetic Order of the Golden Dawn have added celestial correspondences. If *Malkuth* (10) is earth, then:

Yesod	(9) =	the moon
Hod	(8) =	Mercury
Netsah	(7) =	Venus
Tiphereth	(6) =	the sun
Geburah	(5) =	Mars
Hesed	(4) =	Jupiter
Binah	(3) =	Saturn
Hokmah	(2) =	the stars
Kether	(1) =	God as Prime Mover

Each of these spheres was said to be guarded by specific angels and divine beings. Ambitious mystics saw no reason to wait until death before beginning the ascent to God. They claimed the Tree of Life to be a workable scheme for spiritual progress which living individuals can follow. As one ascends, *sefira* by *sefira*, one gains the powers of each, until at last he becomes a god on earth. These powers are trivial, of course, compared to the great spiritual rewards being received, but even so . . .

Thus the way was opened for occultists to pursue the most worldly goals, while convincing themselves of their saintliness. Like alchemy, later kabbalist theory provides a moral smokescreen in which motives are unclear even to their owners. As practiced by members of the Order of the Golden Dawn, the Kabbalah does not seem to have enhanced anyone's spiritual growth. The smokescreen keeps lifting to reveal a choice collection of egomaniacs involved in a hilarious free-for-all.

Israel Regardie, a student of the Golden Dawn in its decline, wrote in 1971: "Whoever one considers in the recent history of the Western secret tradition is almost always an egotist of gigantic proportions, or else an abject Uriah Heep." He urges that a little simple psychotherapy be applied to the loonier followers of the occult.[2]

Those who wish to see the Kabbalah in its true historical perspective will find *Major Trends in Jewish Mysticism* and *On the Kabbalah and Its Symbolism* by Professor Gershom Scholem of the Hebrew University in Jerusalem models of scholarship. Herbert Weiner gives a more personal and wide-ranging view in *9½ Mystics*, which puts even Scholem in perspective.[3] Those determined to study kabbalistic magic should consider Bonewits's advice: begin by learning Hebrew.[4]

Tarot: The Ultimate Rorschach Test

Altogether the Tarots are far too valuable to be con-
fined to mere sorcery, or treated as medieval curiosa. . . .
The cards are the exchange symbols between Inner and
Outer Life, psycho-physical currency convertible into
either dimension.

William Gray, *Magical Ritual Methods*

Playing cards evolved in China—perhaps from chess, domi-
nos, or the paper money of the T'ang dynasty. In Europe
they first appeared in the fourteenth century around the
great seaports of northern Italy, so it is assumed that at least the
idea of playing cards was introduced by Italian merchants, or returning Crusaders. Venice, Pisa, and Genoa had provided supplies
for the Crusaders in the eleventh, twelfth, and thirteenth centuries,
and the Polo brothers of Venice visited China in the late thirteenth
century. Florence, Bologna, Ferrara, and such Lombardian cities as
Milan and Mantua held key positions along the trade routes to eastern France, Flanders, and Germany. At the same time these Italian
cities were in close contact with Spain and southern France, particularly with such centers of learning and translation as Toledo
and Montpellier. Even so, playing cards are not mentioned in sur-

viving records until the late 1300s, roughly a hundred years after the last Crusade. Then one begins to find city ordinances regulating card-playing and descriptions of card games compiled by monks.

Hand-painted cards with recognizable Tarot figures still exist from this period. By the mid-1400s the standard Tarot deck of 78 cards had appeared. Sometimes called the Venetian (or Lombardy or Piedmontese) Tarot, it contained four suits: rods, swords, cups, and coins. A French version called the Marseilles Tarot soon followed and was widely imitated throughout Europe. The familiar suits of today's playing cards evolved directly from the original Tarot suits:

ITALIAN	FRENCH	ENGLISH	
(*Tarot*)	(*Tarot*)	(*Tarot*)	(*Playing Cards*)
Bastoni	Trèfles	Rods (Wands)	Clubs
Spade	Pique	Swords	Spades
Coppe	Coeurs	Cups	Hearts
Denarii	Carreaux	Coins (Disks, Pentacles)	Diamonds

Each Tarot suit contained 10 numbered cards (sometimes called "pips"), plus 4 court cards. These 56 cards (4 × 14) were called the "Minor Arcana" of the Tarot deck. Modern playing cards have dropped one set of court cards (the *cavalli*) and so consist of 52 (4 × 13) cards:

ITALIAN	FRENCH	ENGLISH	
(*Tarot*)	(*Tarot*)	(*Tarot*)	(*Playing Cards*)
Re	Roi	King	King
Dama	Reyne	Queen	Queen
Cavallo	Cavallier	Knight	
Fante	Valet	Page	Jack

PRELUDE TO SCIENCE

In addition to the 56 Minor Arcana cards, Tarot decks contain 22 Major Arcana cards (also called trumps). These symbolic figures seem to have developed independently; exactly when and why they were combined with the Minor Arcana is not known.

However, support for their independent origin is found in fifty didactic engravings made in the Duchy of Ferrara around 1460. Sometimes called *Tarocchi di Mantegna* or *Carte di Baldini*, these were probably designed for study or contemplation rather than for card-playing. They include Apollo and the nine muses, the seven virtues, and thirteen branches of learning (*Grammatica*, *Philosofia*, *Aritmetricha*, and so forth), as well as fifteen figures that are clearly related to the Major Arcana figures of Tarot:

TAROCCHI DI MANTEGNA		TAROT
Misero	I	The Fool
Imperator	VIIII	The Emperor
Papa	X	The Pope (Hierophant)
Astrologia	XXVIIII	Wheel of Fortune
Cosmico	XXXIII	The World
Temperencia	XXXIIII	Temperance
Forteza	XXXVI	Strength
Justicia	XXXVIII	Justice
Luna	XXXXI	The Moon
Mercurio	XXXXII	The Magician
Venus	XXXXIII	The Star / The Lovers
Sol	XXXXIV	The Sun
Marte	XXXXV	The Chariot
Jupiter	XXXXVI	The Pope (Hierophant)
Saturno	XXXXVII	The Hermit

These engravings seem to represent a compendium of Renaissance intellectual themes, rather than a revelation of occult mysteries. Their inclusion in part in the Tarot Major Arcana may help to explain the fascination that Tarot continues to exercise on intellectual writers.

The traditional numbering and titles of the 22 Major Arcana figures are as follows:

	ITALIAN	FRENCH	ENGLISH
0	Il Matto	Le Fou (Le Mat, Le Fol)	The Fool
I	Il Bagatto	Le Bateleur	The Magician
II	La Papessa	La Papesse	The High Priestess (The Female Pope)
III	L'Imperatrice	L'Impératrise	The Empress
IV	L'Imperatore	L'Empéreur	The Emperor
V	Il Papa	Le Pape	The Hierophant (The Pope)
VI	Gli Amanti	L'Amoreux	The Lovers
VII	Il Carro	Le Chariot	The Chariot
VIII	La Giustizia	La Justice	Justice
IX	L'Eremità	L'Ermite (Le Capuchin)	The Hermit
X	Rota di Fortuna	La Roue de Fortune	The Wheel of Fortune
XI	La Forza	La Force	Strength (Fortitude)
XII	Il Penduto	Le Pendu	The Hanged Man
XIII	Il Morte	La Mort	Death
XIV	La Temperanza	La Tempérance	Temperance
XV	Il Diavolo	Le Diable	The Devil
XVI	La Torre	La Maison de Dieu	The Tower
XVII	La Stella	L'Étoile	The Star
XVIII	La Luna	La Lune	The Moon
XIX	Il Sole	Le Soleil	The Sun

PRELUDE TO SCIENCE

	ITALIAN	FRENCH	ENGLISH
XX	Il Giudizio	Le Jugement	The Last Judgement
XXI	Il Mondo	Le Monde	The World

In some decks the Death cards was left untitled. The Pope and the Popess were sometimes metamorphosed into Jupiter and Juno in response to complaints from religious authorities.

Despite the heavily symbolic Major Arcana, Tarot decks were made and used primarily for recreation. Many of the original Tarot games are still played today: a form of pinochle called *tarocco*, for example. In addition Tarot cards must always have lent themselves to fortune-telling. They were already common in Europe when large numbers of Gypsies first appeared there but the Gypsies and their clients soon became attached to them. Although there are countless ways of spreading the cards—some requiring the entire deck and prodigies of interpretation—one of the oldest and simplest is the five-card "astrological" spread:

Card 1 represents the ascendant (conditions that are approaching), card 2 is the descendant (conditions passing away), card 3 is the mid-heaven (conditions prevailing at present), card 4 is the nadir (conditions hidden in the future), and card 5 is the key to the entire spread, the synthesis.

The sturdy woodblock prints of the Marseilles Tarot have been reproduced virtually unchanged century after century and still sell briskly today. They make a useful standard against which to compare recent innovations. For the last two hundred years, occultists have found the urge to rearrange, redesign, or otherwise "fix up" Tarot cards impossible to resist.

Tarot: The Ultimate Rorschach Test

The trend began in the eighteenth century, when the theory was advanced that Tarot cards are not vulgar fortune-telling implements, but the vehicles of Egyptian learning dating back to the pyramids. France was the birthplace of this theory. Shortly before the French Revolution, an amateur scholar and high-degree Mason named Antoine Court de Gébelin wrote a lengthy treatise, *Le Monde Primitif analysé et comparé avec le monde moderne*. In Volume 8 he dealt with *Le Jeu de Tarots* and made a number of sensational claims which no amount of evidence to the contrary will ever banish from occultist belief. Foremost among them are:

Tarot cards were invented by the ancient Egyptians and contain all the most profound and secret wisdom of that civilization.
In the ancient Egyptian language the word "Tarot" means "Royal Road of Life."
Gypsies are direct descendants of the ancient Egyptians.[1]

One must remember that the Rosetta stone which led to the deciphering of Egyptian hieroglyphic writing was not discovered until 1799, so that Egypt was far more mysterious to people of the eighteenth century than it is to us. Gébelin's ideas were taken up by a successful Parisian fortune-teller operating under the name of Etteilla (the reverse of his real name, Alliette). Etteilla claimed that the Tarot deck was really *The Book of Thoth* dictated by Hermes Trismegistus himself and written down on leaves of gold by seventeen Egyptian magicians in a temple near Memphis. His own Tarot deck, in which he maintained he had "restored" the original Egyptian designs, featured curious interpolations and arbitrary changes of meaning and associations. Yet they must have been effective aids in telling fortunes—for which he charged twenty-four *livres*, about five dollars. His deck included cards that represented a Lack of Organization (*Manque d'Ordre*), Boredom (*Ennui*), a Blonde Girl (*Fille Blonde*), Nothingness (*Néant*), and Pregnancy (*Grossesse*).

The cards are still in print and no doubt still shaking up clients all over the world.

Etteilla was the first to present scraps of kabbalistic lore in popular writings on the occult, which stimulated interest in the subject among nonscholars. However, he did not make a connection between the Kabbalah and Tarot. That was the work of another Frenchman, Alphonse-Louis Constant (1810–1875), the giant of nineteenth-century occultism.

Constant studied for the priesthood but abandoned it one week before his final ordination. After a period of sexual and political experimentation, he devoted the remainder of his life to the study of magic. Knowing Hebrew, he was able to go more deeply into the Kabbalah than other gentile occultists could. He adopted a Hebrew version of his name, which he kept until his death. As "Eliphas Levi Zahed," he wrote *Dogme et Rituel de la Haute Magie* [2] and a dozen other works whose influence is still being felt. Aleister Crowley so admired and respected these writings that he managed to convince himself he was Eliphas Levi's reincarnation.

Levi's most original contribution was a systematic linking of Tarot with the Kabbalah. He equated the 4 Tarot suits with the 4 letters of the tetragrammaton: *yodh* = rods (fire), *he* = cups (water), *vau* = swords (air), *he* = disks (earth). He connected the 10 numbered cards in each of the 4 suits to the 10 *sefirot* of the Tree of Life. The 22 Major Arcana cards represented the 22 paths of the Tree and the 22 letters of the Hebrew alphabet.

These correspondences are the basis for nearly all current treatises on Tarot. The authors usually make minor changes in Levi's system and design their own cards (representing them as dazzling creative breakthroughs). But whether or not he is mentioned in these works, Eliphas Levi is still their chief author.

Since he felt obliged to keep the occult "occult," one cannot always be sure when Levi is being truthful and when he is covering his tracks. He used the traditional numbering of the Major Arcana cards and the regular sequence of the Hebrew alphabet, so that The Magician (I) = *aleph*, The High Priestess (II) = *beth*, The Empress (III) = *gimel*, and so forth. However, he inserted the unnumbered card, The Fool (0), between cards XX and XXI, so as to make it correspond with the letter *shin*, a symbol of fire. This system was incorporated in *The Tarot of the Bohemians* by Levi's disciple Gérard Encausse (1865–1917), published under the pseudonym Papus.[3]

The Hermetic Order of the Golden Dawn rejected this for a simpler sequence:

The Fool (0) = *aleph*

The Magician (I) = *beth*

The High Priestess (II) = *gimel* . . .

The Golden Dawn also interchanged the positions of Strength and Justice from XI and VIII to VIII and XI. Wildly eclectic, the Golden Dawn made heroic efforts to tie all occult systems together in one grand supersystem. Justice with its scales suggested the astrological sign Libra, while Strength with its Lion suggested Leo. By changing the positions of these two cards, the signs of the Zodiac could be kept in their normal sequence:

aleph	The Fool (0)	Air
beth	The Magician (I)	Mercury
gimel	The High Priestess (II)	Moon
daleth	The Empress (III)	Venus
he	The Emperor (IV)	Aries
vau	The Hierophant (V)	Taurus
zayin	The Lovers (VI)	Gemini
cheth	The Chariot (VII)	Cancer

teth	Strength (VIII)	Leo
yodh	The Hermit (IX)	Virgo
caph	The Wheel of Fortune (X)	Jupiter
lamed	Justice (XI)	Libra
mem	The Hanged Man (XII)	Water
nun	Death (XIII)	Scorpio
samekh	Temperance (XIV)	Sagittarius
ayin	The Devil (XV)	Capricorn
pe	The Tower (XVI)	Mars
sadh	The Star (XVII)	Aquarius
koph	The Moon (XVIII)	Pisces
resh	The Sun (XIX)	Sun
shin	The Last Judgement (XX)	Fire
tav	The World (XXI)	Saturn

Each letter and card corresponded to a specific path in the Tree of Life, was associated with certain plants and animals, and had its own special color. To embody this system, the Golden Dawn prepared its own Tarot cards.

A Golden Dawn member, Arthur Edward Waite, in 1910 published *The Pictorial Key to the Tarot* with seventy-eight cards drawn and colored by Pamela Colman Smith under his direction. Waite did not reveal all the Golden Dawn's secrets but only "as much as may be expected or required in those outer circles where the qualifications of special research cannot be expected." [4] He wrote in a sneering tone that alienates readers just as he himself alienated his fellow members of the Golden Dawn. Yet the Waite-Smith deck is an original creation and has been extremely influential. Today most writers on Tarot condemn Waite, while at the same time plagiarizing freely from his work.

Up until this time, the "pips" of the Minor Arcana—the ten numbered cards of the four suits—had been drawn much as they

Inc. and distributed by many department stores. Its seventy-eight fuzzed-up vulgarizations of the Waite-Smith cards are a potent argument for strengthening the copyright laws. "Your future is in good hands with the Tarot," warbles the J. C. Penney catalogue hopefully.

A totally new departure is C. C. Zain's Egyptian Tarot deck, which abounds in lotus columns, ankhs, uraei, pyramids, triple crowns, scarabs, and papyri. The Empress is transformed into Isis Unveiled, The Last Judgement becomes The Sarcophagus. Zain's followers Doris Doan and King Keyes in their book *How to Read Tarot Cards* promise a variety of benefits: creativity, enlightenment, perhaps even "an amazing transformation of your personality," influential friends, "to say nothing of the harmonious exchange you can enjoy with your mate." [8]

A significantly original Tarot deck was produced in 1944 by Lady Frieda Harris under the direction of Aleister Crowley. These seventy-eight paintings are so striking and bizarre that they are suitable chiefly for meditation, or for study along with Crowley's *Book of Thoth*. Yet one occasionally finds them being used with apparent success by Tarot card readers on the streets of Berkeley, California. They are a rich mélange of occult symbolism, audaciously expressed.

In the *Book of Thoth*, Crowley makes a more equitable distribution of the sexes by turning the pages into princesses. He also demotes the kings to princes and makes the knights the dominant court cards. Confusion can be avoided by remembering that the knights are always represented on or with a horse as "power in motion," while the princes (ex-kings) occupy a chariot and throne as "established power." Crowley follows the Golden Dawn correspondences, except that he interchanges The Star and The Emperor, so that the Star is linked with the letter *he* and The Emperor with the letter *sadh*. [9]

are in ordinary playing cards; for example, the Nine of Cups simply showed nine cups more or less artistically arranged. The Waite-Smith deck, however, incorporates these symbols in original pictures expressing the divinatory meaning of each card; the Nine of Cups shows a plump contented man sitting with his arms folded before a shelf of nine cups. Thus forty new images have been added to the Tarot deck.

A facsimile of the original Waite-Smith deck (perversely known as the Rider deck, after its first publisher) is still being sold. Another edition features the Smith drawings vividly colored by a different artist, Frankie Albano, with each suit showing a predominant color.

In 1929 another Golden Dawn member, Paul Case, had the Waite-Smith Major Arcana redrawn with minor variations and with the corresponding Hebrew letter included on each card. This represents a sincere attempt to correct Waite's errors and continues to be popular. Unfortunately, what it gained in esoteric "correctness" it lost as art, and some of the cards look like parodies of the originals. [5]

Other variants of the Waite-Smith deck are on the market. The Aquarian Tarot deck features subdued colors, a unified style, and undeniable "good taste." Cruder natures may find it bland and unevocative. This deck is the basis of *The Windows of Tarot* by F. D. Graves. He favors the ancient Egypt theory of Tarot origin and claims to see enormous differences between the Aquarian deck and the Waite-Smith deck. [6]

David Sheridan has designed a Tarot deck that is used in Alfred Douglas's excellent book *The Tarot: The Origins, Meaning and Uses of the Cards*. The drawings are frothy and vivacious and include original designs as well as reworkings of the Waite-Smith designs. [7]

There is nothing original in a deck published by Hoi Polloi

Cosmico (genius of the world), *Tarocchi di Mantegna*, c. 1460. *Courtesy National Gallery of Art, Washington, D.C.*

The World, Marseilles Tarot, original design c. 1500 (modern edition). *Reproduced by permission of U.S. Games Systems Inc., New York, N.Y.*

The only other new Tarot designs—and these are for the Major Arcana cards only—were painted by John Cooke as directed by ouija board in 1962–1963. They are interesting and sexy and have little connection with the older figures they are intended to replace. They are designed for the Aquarian Age, which Cooke and Rosalind Sharpe, authors of *The New Tarot*, believe began November 17, 1959, when the Great Pyramid prophecies ended.[10]

The New Tarot is endorsed by Dr. Ralph Metzner as "another of the increasing numbers of rays of wisdom-light in the fast-accreting darkness of our unfortunate age." [11] He recommends using only the Major Arcana cards when consulting the Tarot. This means that in a routine five-card spread one might receive The World, Death, The Sun, The Devil, and The Last Judgement, or, in the New Tarot, The Virgin, The Renewer, The Doer, The Thinker, and The Knower—both rather portentous readings for a day whose major event may be a visit to the supermarket.

After dictating the twenty-two new cards, Cooke's ouija board announced complacently: "The press has loosed a goodly juice . . . The grape is no longer needed—not even for mash." [12]

Anyone planning to study Tarot should take his time in selecting the deck to use. One tends to favor the first Tarot deck one gets to know—much as one favors the first recording of a symphony one gets to know—and can easily conclude that this is the only "correct" interpretation. Stuart R. Kaplan's *Tarot Classic* presents, without bias, a great variety of Tarot decks, along with an excellent bibliography.[13] The author is president of U.S. Games Systems, Inc., and is also a formidable collector.

Kabbalistic and Egyptian mystery theories dominate the Tarot literature today, but an older, less intellectual tradition is still in operation. For centuries cards have been used for fortune-telling—a vaguely numerological method, always personal, and chiefly about

The World, Waite-Smith ("Rider") Tarot, 1910. *Reproduced by permission of U.S. Games Systems Inc., New York, N.Y.*

The Universe, Crowley-Harris Tarot, 1944. *Courtesy Ordo Templi Orientis, Dublin, California*

money and love. An unexpected gift, a quarrel, a love affair, a delayed marriage, a handsome stranger, death: this is the sort of information Carmen and her friends looked for in the card scene of Bizet's opera. Presenting such information in a plausible fashion while at the same time responding to clues in the client's behavior is a distinct art. Some idea of it can be obtained from writer Basil Rakoczi's monograph, *Fortune Telling*. A final grouping of three cards (the last of eight)

Three of Spades (Swords) = Sorrow
Two of Diamonds (Coins) = Change
Six of Hearts (Cups)　　 = Pleasure; the past influencing the future

is interpreted by his card reader as follows:

> I am looking far ahead. There is street fighting. You rise to power. I see it all. What success! What intrigue! That fine house and the grand marriage . . . but then the tears. Yes, you will look back and see the heart that you have broken. Your own heart will at last begin to ache. Is it all worth it, sir? Stop and think *now*. The fates can be wooed, destiny may change. We have to believe that which we do. Change now, seek another path, triumph over your weaknesses. Yes, you have it in you to be more noble than your cards would make you out to be. Surmount your character weaknesses. *This you know you can do!* [14]

Obviously this is an interpretation that goes far beyond the conventional meanings of the cards and shows a lively creative imagination at work. Emotionally delivered by a magnetic sage in a murky, highly charged setting, it could hardly fail to impress a client. As often noted, the talent of the diviner is more important than the method of divination.

A case can be made for the view that Tarot cards are psychologically useful, that they have diagnostic value, that they are in fact a kind of super Rorschach test, offering seventy-eight vivid images in place of a few ink blots. Tarot cards are used in this way now—and probably always have been. Even people who believe they are contacting "other beings" through Tarot may actually be contacting areas of their own minds.

As with all do-it-yourself psychotherapies, there is an element of risk, but there seems to be plenty of risk in even the most conventional psychoanalytic techniques. In this regard, the effects of drugs on Tarot card readings is instructive.

No doubt alcoholic Tarot card readers exist, but there is a strong tradition that alcohol (except for a token amount of brandy) is not helpful in the process. Psychedelic drugs, on the other hand, are powerfully stimulating and often lead to interminable Tarot sessions with debatable results. One should remember that drugs and divination are closely associated in many primitive societies. The hallucinogenic jungle vine *Banisteriopsis* is brewed by Indians of the Upper Amazon River as an aid to divination; their skill is such that chemists have named one of the vine's psychoactive alkaloids (1-methyl-7-methoxy-B-carboline) "telepathine."

To what extent does Tarot have anything to do with astrology and the Kabbalah? Is it really useful to cram them into one huge syncretic scheme?

Such schemes often show intellectual daring and may produce surprising results, but they also bristle with meaningless juxtapositions and inconsistencies that no amount of revision can cure. The designers of such schemes never seem to benefit from or even to use the schemes themselves. Syncretism is an organizing, intellectual activity that has little to do with the intuitive parts of the mind, although the results in occultism are often as illogical as anyone could wish.

(109)

REFERENCE NOTES

INDEX

REFERENCE NOTES

1. Prelude to What?

1. William Whewell, *The Philosophy of the Inductive Sciences Founded upon Their History* (London: Longmans Green, 1840), p. *cxiii.*
2. Jacques Ellul, *The Technological Society*, trans. John Wilkinson (New York: Knopf, 1964), p. 18.
3. John Burnet, *Early Greek Philosophy*, 4th ed. (London: Adam & Charles Black, 1930), p. *v.*
4. Benjamin Farrington, *Greek Science* (Baltimore: Penguin Books, 1961), p. 311.
5. George Thomson, *The Inspiration of Science* (London: Oxford University Press, 1961), p. 1.
6. Albert Einstein, *Out of My Later Years* (New York: Philosophical Library, 1950), p. 59.
7. T. H. Huxley, "On the Educational Value of the Natural Sciences," in *Collected Essays* (New York: Appleton, 1894), p. 45.
8. P. B. Medawar, *The Art of the Soluble* (London: Methuen, 1967), p. 87.
9. John G. Kemeny, *A Philosopher Looks at Science* (Princeton, N.J.: Van Nostrand, 1959), pp. 175–176.

10. R. H. Bube, *The Encounter Between Science and Christianity* (Grand Rapids, Mich.: W. B. Eerdmans, 1967).
11. James B. Conant, *Science and Common Sense* (New Haven, Conn.: Yale University Press, 1951), pp. 23, 25.
12. Gilbert Lewis, *The Anatomy of Science* (New Haven, Conn.: Yale University Press, 1926), p. 7.

2. *Seven Ways of Not Being Scientific*

1. Jacques Barzun, *The American University* (New York: Harper & Row, 1968), pp. 145–146.
2. Jacques Barzun, *The House of Intellect* (New York: Harper & Row, 1959), p. 21.
3. John G. Kemeny, *A Philosopher Looks at Science* (Princeton, N.J.: Van Nostrand, 1959).
4. "Competitive Problems in the Drug Industry," *Hearings before the Senate Subcommittee on Monopoly*, 90th Congress 1967–1968, Part 10.
5. Joseph F. Coates, quoted in "Science Tilts with Irrationalism," *Chemical and Engineering News*, 15 January 1973.
6. Gerald Holton, "The False Images of Science," in *The Mystery of Matter*, ed. L. B. Young (London: Oxford University Press, 1965).
7. Malachi Martin, "The Scientist as Shaman," *Harper's*, March 1972.
8. Charles Darwin, *Autobiography*, ed. Nora Barlow (London: Collins, 1958).
9. Sir James Frazer, *The New Golden Bough*, ed. T. H. Gaster (New York: Criterion Books, 1959), p. 738.
10. Lucien Lévy-Bruhl, *How Natives Think* (New York: Washington Square Press, 1966; trans. L. A. Clare from *Les Fonctions Mentales dans les Sociétés Inférieures*, Paris, 1910).
11. Claude Lévi-Strauss, *The Savage Mind* (Chicago: University of Chicago Press, 1966; trans. of *La Pensée Sauvage*, Paris: Librairie Plon, 1962), p. 13.

12. Stanislav Andreski, *The Social Sciences as Sorcery* (London: André Deutsch, 1972), p. 11.

3. *Magic: Premonitions of an Unborn Science?*

1. Jean Henri Fabre, "Le Sphex à Ailes Jaunes," *Souvenirs Entomologiques* I (Paris: Librairie Delagrave, 1879), chapter VI.
2. V. Gordon Childe, "The Prehistory of Science: Archeological Documents," *Journal of World History* I:4, 1953; II:1, 1955.
3. *The Papyrus Ebers*, trans. B. Ebbell (Copenhagen: Levin & Munksgaard, 1937).
4. John Anthony West and Jan Gerhard Toonder, *The Case for Astrology* (1970; reprint, Baltimore: Penguin Books, 1973), p. 22.
5. Ralph Metzner, *Maps of Consciousness* (New York: Collier Books, 1971), pp. 87–89, 102–104.
6. Sir James Frazer, *The New Golden Bough*, ed. T. H. Gaster (New York: Criterion Books, 1959), p. 35.
7. Bronislaw Malinowski, *Magic, Science and Religion* (New York: Doubleday, 1922), p. 70.
8. Paul Fejos, "Magic, Witchcraft and Medical Theory," in Iago Goldston, ed., *Man's Image in Medicine and Anthropology* (New York: International Universities Press, 1963).
9. H. R. Schoolcraft, *Archives of Aboriginal Knowledge* (Philadelphia: Lippincott, 1865), vol. 5.
10. William Bradford, *History of the Plimouth Plantation* (1856; reprint, Boston: Wright & Potter, 1901).
11. O. K. Moore, "Divination—a New Perspective," *American Anthropologist* 59:69–74, 1957.
12. E. M. Butler, *Ritual Magic* (Cambridge: The University Press, 1949).
13. Maud Gonne MacBride, *A Servant of the Queen: Her Own Story* (1938; reprint, Dublin: Gold Eagle Books, 1950).
14. M. Levaillant, *La Crise Mystique de Victor Hugo* (Paris: Corti, 1954).

15. Leonard Huxley, *Life and Letters of T. H. Huxley* (New York: Appleton, 1900), p. 453.
16. P. E. I. Bonewits, *Real Magic* (New York: Coward, McCann & Geoghegan, 1971).
17. Butler, *Ritual Magic*, p. 316.
18. Weston La Barre, *The Peyote Cult* (New York: Schocken Books, 1969), p. *xiii*.

4. Divination: Who Knows What the Future Will Bring?

1. E. M. Forster, *Aspects of the Novel* (London: Edward Arnold, 1927).
2. *Lemegeton*, abridged by Sayed Idries Shah in *The Secret Lore of Magic* (1957; reprint, New York: Citadel Press, 1970).
3. Cicero, *De Divinatione*, ed. and trans. W. A. Falconer (London: Loeb Classical Library, 1923).
4. Callisthenes, quoted by Cicero in *De Divinatione*.
5. Cicero, *De Divinatione*.
6. Edward Gibbon, *History of the Decline and Fall of the Roman Empire*, ed. J. B. Bury (London: Methuen, 1897), chapter 2.
7. Richard Wilhelm, *The I Ching, or Book of Changes*, trans. from the German by C. F. Baynes (Princeton, N.J.: Princeton University Press, 1950); Alfred Douglas, *The Oracle of Change* (1971; reprint, Harmondsworth, England: Penguin Books, 1972).
8. Stephen Gaskin, *Monday Night Class* (Berkeley, Calif.: Book People, 1970).
9. Tom Wolfe, *The Electric Kool-Aid Acid Test* (New York: Farrar, Straus and Giroux, 1968), p. 27.
10. Aleister Crowley, *Magick in Theory and Practice* (1929; reprint, New York: Castle Books, 1960).
11. Joseph Needham, *Science and Civilization in China* (Cambridge: Cambridge University Press, 1956).

12. René Dubos, *The Mirage of Health* (New York: Harper & Bros., 1959).
13. Gustav Jahoda, *The Psychology of Superstition* (Harmondsworth, England: Penguin Books, 1969), p. 147.
14. Bronislaw Malinowski, *Magic, Science and Religion* (New York: Doubleday, 1922), p. 90.
15. Ray Hyman and Evon Z. Vogt, *Water Witching U.S.A.* (Chicago: University of Chicago Press, 1959).

5. *Astrology: Are We Fools by Heavenly Compulsion?*

1. Ake Wallenquist, *Dictionary of Astronomical Terms*, trans. Sune Engelbrektson (New York: Natural History Press, 1966).
2. O. Neugebauer and H. B. Van Hoesen, *Greek Horoscopes* (Philadelphia: American Philosophical Society, 1959).
3. Ibid.
4. Benjamin Farrington, *Greek Science* (Baltimore: Penguin Books, 1961), pp. 13–14.
5. E. J. Bickerman, *Chronology of the Ancient World* (Ithaca, N.Y.: Cornell University Press, 1968).
6. *Explanatory Supplement to the Astronomical Ephemeris* (London: Her Majesty's Stationery Office, 1961).
7. Hesiod, *Works and Days*, ed. H. G. Evelyn-White (London: Loeb Classical Library, 1936).
8. Pliny the Elder, *Natural History*, ed. H. H. Rackham (London: Loeb Classical Library), Books II (1949) and XVIII (1950).
9. D. R. Dicks, *Early Greek Astronomy to Aristotle* (Ithaca, N.Y.: Cornell University Press, 1970), p. 165.
10. Hesiod, *Works and Days*.
11. Pliny, *Natural History*.
12. Claudius Ptolemy, *Tetrabiblos*, ed. F. E. Robbins (London: Loeb Classical Library, 1940), p. 357.

6. The Mechanics of Traditional Astrology

1. André Barbault, *Le Zodiaque*, 12 v. (1957–1959), *Traité Pratique d'Astrologie* (1961), *De la Psychoanalyse à l'Astrologie* (1961) (Paris: Editions du Seuil).
2. Dane Rudhyar, *The Pulse of Life* (1963; reprint, Berkeley, Calif.: Shambala Publications, 1970).

7. Making Astrology "Scientific"

1. John Anthony West and Jan Gerhard Toonder, *The Case for Astrology* (1970; reprint, Baltimore: Penguin Books, 1973), p. 142.
2. Marc Edmund Jones, *How to Learn Astrology* (1941; reprint, New York: Doubleday, 1971), p. 52.
3. Marc Edmund Jones, *Astrology* (1945; reprint, Baltimore: Penguin Books, 1971), p. 131.
4. Dane Rudhyar, *The Astrology of Personality* (1936; reprint, New York: Doubleday, 1970), p. *xi*.
5. Rupert Gleadow, *The Zodiac Revealed* (London: Dent, 1968).
6. Steven Schmidt, *Astrology 14: Your New Sun Sign* (New York: Bobbs-Merrill, 1970), p. 12.
7. William H. Sheldon, *The Varieties of Human Physique* (New York: Harper & Bros., 1940), and *The Varieties of Human Temperament* (New York: Harper & Bros., 1942).
8. Martin A. Pomerantz, *Cosmic Rays* (New York: Van Nostrand–Reinhold, 1971).
9. Albert P. Krueger and Richard F. Smith, "The Biological Mechanisms of Air Ion Action. I. 5-Hydroxytryptamine as the Endogenous Mediator of Positive Air Ion Effects on the Mammalian Trachea," *Journal of General Physiology* 43:533–540, 1960; Richard F. Smith and Wallace H. Fuller, "Identification and Mode of Action of a Component of Positively-Ionized Air Causing Enhanced Growth in Plants," *Plant Physiology* 36: 747–751, 1961.

10. Michel Gauquelin, *L'Astrologie devant la Science* (Paris: Editions Planète, 1966; trans. James Hughes as *The Scientific Basis of Astrology: Myth or Reality?* New York: Stein & Day, 1969); Andrija Puharich, *Beyond Telepathy* (New York: Doubleday, 1962); René Dubos, *Man Adapting* (New Haven, Conn.: Yale University Press, 1965).

11. Carl Jung, *Synchronicity, Collected Works,* vol. VIII (Princeton, N.J.: Princeton University Press, 1969); Carl Jung and Wolfgang Pauli, *The Interpretation of Nature and the Psyche* (London: Kegan Paul, 1955).

12. Gustav Jahoda, *The Psychology of Superstition* (Harmondsworth, England: Penguin Books, 1969), p. 14.

8. Has Astrology Value?

1. Alan Watts, *In My Own Way* (New York: Pantheon Books, 1972), p. 11.

2. Leo Rosten, *The Joys of Yiddish* (New York: McGraw-Hill, 1968).

3. J. B. S. Haldane, *Science and Everyday Life* (London: Lawrence & Wishart, 1939).

4. Aldous Huxley, *Crome Yellow* (New York: Harper & Bros., 1922).

5. John Anthony West and Jan Gerhard Toonder, *The Case for Astrology* (1970; reprint, Baltimore: Penguin Books, 1973).

9. The Kabbalah: Letters and Numbers of Power

1. *The Zohar,* trans. Harry Sperling and Maurice Simon (London: Soncino Press, 1931–1934).

2. Israel Regardie, *My Rosicrucian Adventure,* 2nd ed. (Saint Paul, Minn.: Llewellyn Publications, 1971), p. 4.

3. Gershom Scholem, *Major Trends in Jewish Mysticism* (New York:

Schocken Books, 1954); and *On the Kabbalah and Its Symbolism* (New York: Schocken Books, 1965); Herbert Weiner, *9½ Mystics: The Kabbala Today* (New York: Holt, Rinehart and Winston, 1969).

4. P. E. I. Bonewits, *Real Magic* (New York: Coward, McCann and Geoghegan, 1971).

10. Tarot: The Ultimate Rorschach Test

1. Antoine Court de Gébelin, *Le Monde Primitif, analysé et comparé avec le monde moderne,* 9 vols. (Paris, 1775–1784), vol. 8.

2. Eliphas Lévi, *Dogme et Rituel de la Haute Magie* (Paris: Baillière, 1854; trans. A. E. Waite as *Transcendental Magic,* reprint, London: Rider, 1968).

3. Papus (Gérard Encausse), *The Tarot of the Bohemians, Absolute Key to Occult Science* (1889; reprint, London: Rider, 1919).

4. Arthur Edward Waite, *The Pictorial Key to the Tarot (Being Fragments of a Secret Tradition Under the Veil of Divination)* (London: Rider, 1910).

5. Paul Foster Case, *The Tarot: A Key to the Wisdom of the Ages* (1929; reprint, Richmond, Va.: Macoy Publishing, 1947).

6. F. D. Graves, *The Windows of Tarot* (Dobbs Ferry, N.Y.: Morgan & Morgan, 1973).

7. Alfred Douglas, *The Tarot: The Origins, Meaning and Uses of the Cards* (London: Victor Gollancz, 1973).

8. Doris Chase Doane and King Keyes, *How to Read Tarot Cards* (1967; reprint, New York: Funk & Wagnalls, 1968).

9. Aleister Crowley, *The Book of Thoth* (1944; reprint, New York: Lancer Books, 1971).

10. John Cooke and Rosalind Sharpe, *The New Tarot: The Tarot for the Aquarian Age* (Kentfield, Calif.: Western Star Press, 1968).

11. Ibid., introduction by Ralph Metzner, p. *iv.*

12. Cooke and Sharpe, *The New Tarot,* p. 137.

13. Stuart R. Kaplan, *Tarot Classic* (New York: Grosset and Dunlap, 1972).
14. Basil Rakoczi, *Fortune Telling* (London: Macdonald Unit 75, 1970), p. 35.

INDEX

Abracadabra, 85
Age of Aquarius, 68
Agriculture
  and magic, 20
  and star movements, 44–45, 47–48
Agrippa, Cornelius, 88
Air
  as an element, 17, 54, 55
  ionized, 17–18, 77–79
  and zodiac signs, 54, 55
Albano, Frankie, 101
Alchemy
  and chemistry, 16–17
  as a spiritual discipline, 17–18, 50, 91
Ammon, oracle of, 27
Andreski, Stanislav, 13–14
Anti-science, 11–12
Apollo, 26
Aristotle, 14, 54

Art, 4, 8, 18
Ascendant, 57
Aspects, 61–63, 74
Astrological terms
  ascendant, 57
  aspects, 62–63, 74
  horoscopes, 39–40, 51–65
  houses, 57–62, 74
  mundane astrology, 39
  natal astrology, 39
  progressions, 63
  sun sign, 57
  transits, 63
Astrology, 11, 13, 36–84
  and astronomy, 16–17, 36–40, 51–52
  horoscopes, 39–40, 51–65
  and ionized air, 77–79
  mechanics of, 50–65
  objections to: religious and social, 81–83; scientific, 66–80

(123)

INDEX

ABOUT THE AUTHOR

Richard Furnald Smith received his B.S. in chemistry in 1950, his M.S. in biochemistry in 1952, and his Ph.D. in biochemistry in 1962, all from the University of Arizona. Formerly a research biochemist with the Forest Service of the United States Department of Agriculture, he is currently teaching at the University of California Extension at Berkeley. *Prelude to Science* grew out of a course which he taught there. He is also the author of *Chemistry for the Million.*